"Rick Bundschuh has done it again w. One minute, I find myself giggling wit. seconds, I'm pulling the dagger out of for loving the church but not being afra ......ging ner course."

—Dr. David Olshine
director of student ministries,
Columbia International University, Columbia, SC

"What a fun and exciting book this is! If you only read chapter 12, you get your money's worth. Actually every chapter is a gem—each one full of wonderful and dangerous ideas that make me wish I had a key to Rick's church. (Read chapter 10 and you'll wish you had one, too.)

—Wayne Rice
director, Understanding Your Teenager; co-founder, Youth Specialties

"In a day when many people are hopelessly dissatisfied with "organized religion" and are fleeing the church, we need help. As an outside-the-box pastor, speaker, and author, Rick Bundschuh has reminded us that the problem isn't with the church, but rather with us! We need to be changed—in our thinking, in our delivery of God's life-giving message of hope and healing, and in the way we "do" church. This is a real, practical, and helpful tool."

—Chap Clark
Ph.D., associate professor of youth, family, and culture, Fuller Theological Seminary

"I mean it: anyone who loves the church should read this book. Rick Bundschuh not only loves the church, but he loves it enough to not let it get comfortable. He lives what he teaches and has the scars to prove it. This book is prophetic, compelling, practical, disturbing and a must read."

—JIM BURNS, PH.D.
Ph.D., president, HomeWord

"Rejuvenating, refreshing, revitalizing for anyone who thinks ministry is boring."

—DAN CHUN
senior pastor, First Presbyterian Church of Honolulu;
president, Hawaiian Islands Ministries

DON'T ROCK THE BOAT, CAPSIZE IT

*Loving the Church Too Much
to Leave It the Way It Is*

By Rick Bundschuh

NAVPRESS®

BRINGING TRUTH TO LIFE

OUR GUARANTEE TO YOU

We believe so strongly in the message of our books that we are making this quality guarantee to you. If for any reason you are disappointed with the content of this book, return the title page to us with your name and address and we will refund to you the list price of the book. To help us serve you better, please briefly describe why you were disappointed. Mail your refund request to: NavPress, P.O. Box 35002, Colorado Springs, CO 80935.

The Navigators is an international Christian organization. Our mission is to reach, disciple, and equip people to know Christ and to make Him known through successive generations. We envision multitudes of diverse people in the United States and every other nation who have a passionate love for Christ, live a lifestyle of sharing Christ's love, and multiply spiritual laborers among those without Christ.

NavPress is the publishing ministry of The Navigators. NavPress publications help believers learn biblical truth and apply what they learn to their lives and ministries. Our mission is to stimulate spiritual formation among our readers.

ISBN 1-57683-646-0

Cover design by The DesignWorks Group, Charles Brock
Cover water image by Getty; preserver image by Photos.com
Creative Team: Nicci Jordan, Traci Mullins, Darla Hightower, Arvid Wallen, Laura Spray

Some of the anecdotal illustrations in this book are true to life and are included with the permission of the persons involved. All other illustrations are composites of real situations, and any resemblance to people living or dead is coincidental.

Unless otherwise identified, all Scripture quotations in this publication are taken from the HOLY BIBLE: NEW INTERNATIONAL VERSION® (NIV®). Copyright © 1973, 1978, 1984 by International Bible Society. Used by permission of Zondervan Publishing House. All rights reserved. Other versions used include: *THE MESSAGE* (MSG). Copyright © 1993, 1994, 1995, 1996, 2000, 2001, 2002. Used by permission of NavPress Publishing Group.

Bundschuh, Rick, 1951-
  Don't rock the boat, capsize it : loving the church too much to leave
it the way it is / by Rick Bundschuh.
    p. cm.
  Includes bibliographical references.
  ISBN 1-57683-646-0
  1. Church. 2. Church renewal. I. Title.
  BV600.3.B86 2005
  262'.001'7--dc22
                                2004021305

Printed in United States of America

1 2 3 4 5 6 7 8 9 10 / 10 09 08 07 06 05

FOR A FREE CATALOG OF
NAVPRESS BOOKS & BIBLE STUDIES,
CALL 1-800-366-7788 (USA)
OR 1-800-839-4769 (CANADA)

For Tom, Mike, Dain, Doug, Gary, and Creature.

Toad Hall would have been lost long ago without the love, honesty, scolding, and support from you and your families.

CONTENTS

FOREWORD

It is encouraging to see a light of creativity on the dark horizon of status quo. To have it brought into focus for all to see is better yet. Rick's "gospel" is simple: We don't have to be locked in to the common church trend and tradition of mediocrity; change is possible and often necessary. Indeed, we can be vital and refreshingly relevant as the body of Christ in the twenty-first century. In his book, Rick brings fresh, common-sense ideas from theory to fact, from potential to possibility.

I've known Rick since he was a long-haired teenage surfer in Pacific Beach, California. Even as a young teen he was a type A leader, and in a matter of time it became apparent that he wasn't a typical paint-by-the-numbers kind of person. In fact he wasn't typical at all. He was a rare and refreshing species of creative realist with the courage and skill to implement his ideas successfully. Building on a long and successful history in church youth work, Rick became the ringleader of an unusual church in Hawaii that emits a unique and attractive fragrance—another growing example of Rick's practical approach to living and spreading the message of Christ's gospel.

Admittedly this book and its ideas are not for the timid or insecure leader or layperson. Rick shares not only edgy ideas and practical examples of what can be done, but he motivates his readers to release their grip on status quo and careen wildly toward making the church relevant today.

E. G. Von Trutzschler
San Diego, California

ACKNOWLEDGMENTS

A book doesn't just magically appear on the shelf at the local bookstore. Many book concepts are aborted before they get to the runway or linger a slow death trying to find a publisher that believes in the ideas enough to help get them airborne.

I was fortunate to find some book lovers among the fine people of NavPress Publishing Group who were fascinated by my out-of-the-box ideas. A debt of gratitude is also owed to Marko at Youth Specialties, who championed the book based on a few completed chapters and made the important contacts for it to find a home at NavPress.

This book has its genesis in the kindness and goodwill of the people and leadership of Kauai Christian Fellowship who have been such willing subjects for wild experimentation and who allowed me to vacate my post during the time it took to commit the results to paper.

My family also deserves a serious tip of the hat for allowing me to ignore them as crunch time got closer. (And yes, I will be making good on all the "when I get done with this book" promises I made.)

Finally, a huge *mahalo* (no, it does not mean "trash" in Hawaiian even if it is on the lid of all the trash cans) goes to Nicci Jordan, editorial assistant at NavPress, and my editor, Traci Mullins of Eclipse Editorial Services. Thank you for hanging out on the edge with me on this unusual project! You ladies have been upbeat, positive, professional, and an absolute joy to work with. I owe you surfing lessons or something.

God-Induced Wildness

It's a scary world out there.

The secular society has infiltrated the church so effectively that one wonders who is influencing whom. Changes in culture that used to take decades or even centuries to happen now spring upon us in microseconds. New churches pop up in shopping centers and within a few years outstrip in numbers, energy, and vibrancy what some established churches have taken half a century or more to accomplish. Comfortable traditions are being challenged or abandoned. Problems that were once considered a scandal within a Christian community seem almost routine. Pastors fall from grace in a sad, regular rhythm.

With so much uncertainty, it is understandable if our response as Christians is to pull into our own safe, closed community complete with our own language, systems, and hierarchies. After all, most of us find comfort in the rules and particular order of our Christian ghetto. But it's easy, then, to become a fortress locked tight against the world Jesus asked us to penetrate with His love.

Not every church succumbs to the natural urge to hide behind defenses. Some go on the offensive. Some congregations believe in taking risks. Big ones. Some don't fear God-induced wildness. Some have chosen adventure over comfort. Some don't want to be tamed.

Other than some fundamental principles found in the Bible, there are no time-proven templates for what it takes to be a church that penetrates its culture rather than retreats from it or becomes swept up in it. It takes a lot of experimenting and embracing the possibility of failure. It takes a group of believers who are honest enough to admit that the church has often been impotent due to miscalculations, fear of challenge and change, and a desire to stay in a warm and toasty environment. It takes people crazy enough to uncage their lunatic fringe thinkers. It takes people brave enough to suggest that we have built our little Christian boat upside down, and to really get somewhere it won't do just to rock the boat; we must capsize it, and then use creative efforts to get it right side up.

The man who wrote the foreword for this book is the kind of brave soul I'm talking about. "Von" has labored for years among those whom the rest of the church routinely ignores. His early ministry was with teens, and even though he couldn't swim he managed to impact the San Diego surfer community for the gospel in a significant way. Surfers are a tough bunch to get to church. I know; I was one of them. Because of Von I came to Christ at the age of sixteen.

A prophetic voice to the church, Von has been years ahead of

his time—so far ahead that people have often ignored his vision-
ary direction. A couple of decades ago Von dedicated himself to
helping the poor people across the border. His outfit, Spectrum
Ministries, is one of the most beloved works among the destitute throng that live in the cracks and crannies of Tijuana. When
children see his car bouncing down the dirt road they run to the
street chanting his name, as if he is "El Presidente" himself. At
seventy-five years old, the man runs circles around younger guys
in ministry and has seen it all.

This book is about what it *feels* like to look at Christianity and
church in an out-of-the-box, even upside-down way—the way
Von has for decades and the way I have for a good stretch now.
In this book I hope to give you a taste of what is experienced at
both the leadership level and the grassroots level when a group of
believers becomes aware that we Christians have a lot of things
backward and tries to turn itself right side up and inside out. The
stories and ideas in the pages ahead reflect the experiences of real
people living out their sometimes difficult and complicated lives
with each other as if they are on a wondrous escapade designed
and orchestrated by God Himself. (What a concept.)

This book is not designed to be *instructive*, or even theoreti-
cal, although you may find God whispering something to you
about His priorities and viewpoint. It is not designed to hoist a
particular church or individuals into prominence. While I will
attempt to illustrate how many of the ideas we've come up with
at Kauai Christian Fellowship are put into practice, I have no
interest in holding up our congregation as some kind of new or
ideal church model to copy. I want people to think for them-

selves, not follow us. Therefore, I will not be offering a specific grid or template. You will not find in these pages the *10 Steps to an Effective Church*, *5 Principles for Becoming a Mega Ministry*, or any other kind of system. Instead, you will find a scrapbook of musings and mumblings, plus lots of examples of church rethink that will hopefully serve as a yank on the light cord of your own imagination.

It may be helpful to give you the context of these ramblings and rants. Just over a dozen years ago, I was dragged kicking and screaming out of my little comfort zone of youth work in a cozy established church and thrust into being part of the leadership team of a new congregation. Not that youth lock-ins were over for me; until recently I still ran most of the youth activities at Kauai Christian Fellowship, but in addition I was helping to oversee the church as a whole.

Our new congregation was youth heavy. There were more quarters and soda pull rings in the offering basket than dollar bills. In fact, in many ways we were a mutant and morphing youth group growing up into being a church. I knew from the start that we would have to rethink how we would "do church" to make it authentic, effective, and compelling to people who have the attention span of rabbits but who also embody savvy and sincerity in their desire to find and express an authentic faith.

So we did things different. Very different.

As a result we attracted, um, *interesting* kinds of people. Not just kids but people of all ages. We collected people who hated going to church; people with really bad habits; people with messy tangled lives; people who obviously had no clue; and people who couldn't find anything in the Bible or even find a Bible.

We made some of them staff members.

Things haven't changed much over the years. About 85 percent of our folks do not come from a church background. We still get more than our fair share of those whom we affectionately call "trolls and varmints." I have no idea if the ideas we cooked up for our strange collection of people will work for any other church in any other geographical location or with any other mix of people. If you find something you like in our experience, please steal it; otherwise my only aspiration is that our journey will make you scratch your head and ponder "what if . . .?"

From experience, I do know that there is nothing more refreshing than abandoning the same old tired approach to many of our church models (that haven't worked very well for years anyhow) and thinking about things from a whole different angle. It's actually a lot of fun to break many of the unspoken rules on how to do church and discover that it's possible to go zipping along without those restraints.

So thank you for coming along for the ride. Make sure to keep your arms in the air, scream so as to annoy your neighbor, and please don't bother clinging to the gunwales. We aren't just rockin', we are rotating all the way over!

Rick Bundschuh
Kauai, Hawaii

CHAPTER 1

Where Good Things Run Wild

Making Room for an Invigorating Faith

Chesterton. What a guy.

I have a photo of the corpulent British intellectual dressed as a Wild West gunslinger slouching next to famed atheist Bertrand Russell, who is also dressed as a gunslinger.

G. K. Chesterton was always a much better aim than Russell in a verbal shoot-out. Nearly a hundred years later, his barbs and observations can pack more of a wallop than those of most contemporary thinkers. So I stole the title of this chapter from a book of Chesterton's called *Orthodoxy*.

And the more I considered Christianity, the more I found that while it had established a rule and order, the chief aim of that order was to give room for good things to run wild.

It seems to me that most people who are leading and attending churches have gotten the "rule and order" part down but are scared to death of the "run wild" part. And yet it's the wild, dangerous, and challenging part of Christianity that is active and invigorating!

Now don't get me wrong; I'm not an anarchist. I take solace in rules. I find comfort in order. Rules and order seem to be woven into the fabric of creation. Governments, families, and even churches need them so that things can get done without frustration, clashing agendas, waste, and lunacy.

But sometimes people, especially in churches, get confused about the *intent* of rules and, as a result, get a little rigid, inflexible, or just plain silly. Rules and order are designed to provide a safe context for divine craziness to happen, for good things to run amuck, for dreams to be dreamed and excitement to be born. The problem with rules divorced from their intent is simply that they tend to become an end in themselves rather than the helpmate for imagination and creativity.

While every institution tends to come up with its own conventions and systems, it seems to me that the church is quick to make rules, codes, and formulas—and even quicker to forget why it was that those rules, codes, and formulas were made. They simply become tradition or "the way we've always done it." Sometimes the silliness becomes enshrined as doctrine or even group identity.

Much of the time, rules and policies are born out of fear or a bad experience and are championed by people who relish micromanagement or those who privately love the false security that control offers and who fear the unpredictability of wildness. And often these rules, on the surface, seem sensible or simply a minor intrusion. In reality, the result often heaps unnecessary burdens on those already burdened.

Take, for example, the suggestion to rush to create rules and polices due to an abuse of the copy machine in our church office. One day the office manager came in to find discarded in the trash several photocopies of someone's clothed butt. (Thankfully it was *clothed*.) Now, copying butts was not the purpose of our purchasing the copy machine, and of course paper and toner are expensive. (I estimated that there was at least a nickel's worth of waste in the trash can.)

Some well-meaning folks, outraged that the copy machine had been defiled, recommended that we put a book next to the machine so that those making copies could record the volume and official nature of their use. This, they told us, is what they did at their former church (when presumably renegades copied their butts as well).

On first examination, this seemed like a reasonable rule, a new safeguard policy that would be championed as good stewardship by those who love this kind of utopian micromanagement. But this idea was, like many other "helpful" policy ideas people hatch, a very dumb one that would do little to solve the issue of making copies of one's butt, but go a long way to making more work for everyone else.

Our leadership team gave the suggestion about two seconds of thought and then explained to the well-meaning folks that this approach probably works okay for the moral or compliant folks who are using the machine only for church business—but we had serious doubts that we would find someone recording in the book that they made copies of their butt. So all the book would do is create work for those who are not using the machine for something as bizarre as taking pictures of their backsides . . . which was most everybody.

We also pointed out that someone would have to be appointed to be the book cop to look over the sign-in book to see if there were a violators dumb enough to write down that they copied their rear end, their term paper, an *Opus* newspaper comic, their tax forms, or something not on the approved list, and then bill them for the ten or twenty cents worth of toner and paper they had used.

In the end we made a choice based on what risk we would be willing to take. We decided to face the possibility that we might lose a few bucks to the unscrupulous so that access to the copy machine would be convenient for all who needed it to do ministry. We chose to do without record books, passwords, locks, or any other devices that are meant to protect but really only hinder people from doing their jobs—or worse, give the "we don't trust you" message.

We framed the butt pictures and hung them next to the copy machine.

Allowing good things to run wild does not mean exploring the far reaches of the Pentecostal solar system for the goofiest manifestation of the Spirit. It does not mean throwing overboard good sense, propriety, manners, or biblical integrity. It does mean exploring waters uncharted by most church folks, digging around in the imagination attic, or dusting off neglected ideas in the basement of collective history. It means setting off on new voyages of discovery that, while unusual and uncomfortable at the time, are endowed with purpose, potential, and meaning.

How a wildly good thing gets loose and what it is in particular is not the point; it is that it is allowed to come out in the first place.

A group of mechanically minded men who offer to do free minor repairs for single moms one Saturday a month is a wild and good thing.

A bunch of high school kids who commit to forgo buying soft drinks in order to use that money collectively to support a destitute child for Compassion International is a wild and good thing.

Encouraging people to miss church once in a while in order to play golf (and maybe say a word or two about Jesus) with an unsaved neighbor or friend is a wild and good thing.

Asking everyone to keep their tithes and offerings one Sunday morning and instructing them to use the funds this week to do an act of love, encouragement, or affirmation for another person in the spirit of Christ is a wild and good thing.

Deciding that all the pastoral staff will have the same salary regardless of age, education, or position of ministry is a wild and good thing—especially for the traditionally underpaid youth workers.

Collecting funds and paying for talented musicians in the church to make a recording of their music and then giving CDs for free to the whole congregation is a wild and good thing.

Showing up at a school bus stop (ahead of the bus) on a cold morning with hot chocolate and donuts for all the kids is a wild and good thing.

Turning the church into an art gallery where the efforts of the visually creative types in the congregation can display their works is a wild and good thing.

Telling a parable that is hard to figure out and sending everyone home scratching his head (kind of like Jesus did) is a wild and good thing.

But these are ideas from my little cooker in one small corner of the world. Perhaps in a few chapters you will feel frisky enough to think of a bunch on your own. You could be part of unleashing divine good in your own church and seeing how wildly it runs for the good of all.

CHAPTER 2

"You Guys Are CRAZY!!! (But I Love It!)"

Status Quo Busters

Once I strapped a video camera on a little dog.

It's pretty interesting what the world looks like from a wiener dog's point of view. Lots of ankles, feet, carpet, and wall molding. The grass is taller, the bushes are trees, and the trees are as tall as Jack's beanstalk.

It can really help expand our thinking and quicken our imagination if we can break out of our natural and comfortable environment and see things from a different angle.

It made a pretty cool video too.

Each year we send a group of high school students to a Third World country. We call it a mission trip—but who are we kidding? These kids don't know the language of the country they will be going to, they have no contacts other than the *real* missionaries who will be guiding them around, and who really knows if the pantomime gospel skit they perform will really connect or just get courtesy applause? And everyone will be home in a couple of weeks.

Naw . . . they're not missionaries. Hopefully they've helped out a bit here or there, but the *real* purpose of the experience is to make an impression on the kids, not for the kids to change the Third World country. Hopefully a couple of them will end up offering their lives to the mission field as a result. All I'm sure of is that actually living, working, eating, bathing, and using the restroom in an honest to goodness Third World place will change a sheltered, pampered American kid forever.

So don't think wrong of me if I suggest that a lot of people in the church need to get out more. Especially the "life-ers."

Start by going to a completely different church. If you are black, go to a staid, upper-crust white church. If you are white, go to a rockin', soulful black church. If you come from a charismatic church, check out a traditional Catholic mass. If you are liturgical, find a Pentecostal church to try out.

I have. Each experience was eye opening.

I went to church while on a surf trip to Samoa. They took the offering at the door and asked us our names as we handed over our cash. That's different. At the end of the service the pastor got up and read each person's name *and* the amount he or she had added to the church coffers. That'll sure make people want to give more!

I've been a total stranger in a church so small and ingrown that the congregation sang a few extra rounds of "Just As I Am" just for me in hopes that finally an unbeliever had stumbled into their midst and would grope his way down the aisle to the altar. (Even though I was already a Christian I was tempted to take the walk just so they could all go home happy—or at least just go home.)

Why expose yourself to such a mix of experiences? Because it will enlarge your frame of reference, probably strengthen your faith, possibly get you mad or focused, give you some great stories and maybe a creative idea or two.

Our home Bible study group wanted to learn about different religions. Fair enough. We spent a week or two carefully going over what orthodox Christians believe, and then we invited representatives from other faiths to come and share what they believe and why. The Mormon boys with their white shirts, ties, and hard shoes came and sat among all the T-shirt-clad evangelicals. The fidgety pair of Jehovah's Witnesses who were sure they had stepped into some kind of trap explained why they are right and the rest of Christendom is wrong.

It was great! Of course I had to assure each visiting group that it wasn't an ambush and make sure that any zealot from our camp was on good behavior.

Word got out about this zany Bible study and the host home was packed to the gills each week. At the end of the study none of us had converted to another religion nor did any of our visitors decide to join our church. But we did manage to build a little bridge of goodwill between our church and some of the folks in our community who knew little about genuine Christianity. Now when we cross each other's paths in the supermarket, friendly waves are exchanged. We enjoy good-natured kidding around while waiting to pick up our kids from soccer practice.

There is a subtle art in getting your mind out of the box. There is an electric kind of joy that comes from careening right along the edge of seeming disaster. Most churches are full of people who don't know how to look at what they are doing from another perspective, or they haven't been encouraged to try. If we are willing to stop merely talking about how big our God is and start experiencing His wonder and wildness, we are going to have to learn a few things.

Here are some status quo busters that we've used to get the cerebral juices flowing.

Cook Up the Sacred Cow. Every church has at least one. Have pew races. Play air-soft in the sanctuary. Use the good china for a middle school barbecue.

I recall almost losing my job at one church because my junior high Sunday school class was growing so fast I couldn't supply the kids with enough Bibles. After one Sunday three kids from unchurched homes came up begging for a Bible. I snuck into the sanctuary and swiped three of the special "Given in memorial to:_____" pew Bibles, handed them to the kids, and made them swear they would read the thing every day.

Boy! I ground someone's sacred cow into hamburger that morning! Even my argument that the dearly departed in whose names the Bibles were purchased would probably have preferred they go to some sans-Bible kids who were eager to read it failed to persuade all parties. But it was a great conversation starter in the church for a while. ("Hey, what do ya think of what that crazy youth guy did last Sunday?")

Ask Yourself, "What If . . .?" What if we changed the whole configuration of the seating each Sunday? What if we messed with the order of our service? What if we served near-beer at the church picnic?

My friend Mike asked the question, "What if the church staff behaved like the congregation and decided they'd rather sleep in or goof off instead of going to church on Sunday?" "What if?" turned into "Why not?" and a few weeks later the congregation was shocked to come to church and find a note signed by the pastoral staff saying that they figured what was good for the goose was good for the gander and they'd decided to spend this Sunday taking it easy, and would someone please fill in for them.

Heh, Heh, Heh. Gutsy? Crazy? Memorable? You bet! And the following Sunday when the pastor explained the idea that the church only works the way it's designed to when everyone, from the top down and bottom up, pulls together with the same dedication, the congregation, with the object lesson still in mind, hung on every word.

If your church doesn't seem to be going anywhere, ask, "What if we've got this thing upside down?" And play with what it would look like if it were flipped over.

Experiment with Being a Different Kind of Person. I think it was economist Kenneth Boulding who said, "There are two kinds of people in this world: those who divide everything into two groups and those who don't." For just a minute stop being an adult. Stop (or start) dividing everything into two groups. For just a minute forget that we might get sued or that so and so would be outraged. For a minute pretend that your life has been reduced to carrying all your worldly goods on your back. For a minute discuss an idea as if money were not an object or the pastor would never go for it. Try looking at a concept as a member of the opposite sex, as an awkward, pimply young teen, or as a person with a handicap.

While you are pretending, remember that what God has in store for each of us is exactly this: becoming a different kind of person than we currently are. Becoming more like Jesus. Scary, huh?

Come at Ideas from Another Angle. Reverse it, turn it upside down, look for a back door, explore alternative routes. Dr. Edward Jenner, the man who came up with a cure for smallpox, was able to do so because he stopped trying to figure out a cure and started trying to figure out why some people never seemed to get the disease. This led him to dairymaids, which led him to cow pox, which led to the vaccine that saved lives!

Our job as Christians is to help people come to know Christ and to grow in that relationship with Him. Some of our old ways of doing that just aren't working too well anymore (not that some of them ever did). Perhaps what we need is some fresh thinking on the subject in the direction Dr. Jenner took. Figure out why people don't seem to be getting our message and we are halfway to a solution!

Use Those Who Have the Gift of Imagination. Most of us lived in a world of imagination as kids but somewhere along the line gave it up for the *real* world. Fortunately, some folks escaped through the net. Find a small group of the most creative lights you can, throw them in a room with a problem to solve, things to doodle on, and lots of coffee and munchies and see what happens. Sometimes one really good idea comes out of a whole pile of okay or just zany ideas.

The idea someone had to use some of our spare acreage to grow pumpkins is one of those kind of ideas.

Now this might seem like no big deal in many parts of the country, but on this little rock in the middle of the ocean no one has ever picked out a Halloween pumpkin at any place but the grocery store. We grow lots of fruit, cane, and even corn—but no pumpkins. So when one of our green-thumb types offered to clear and plant the empty lot with pumpkins that would be ready to be picked in time for the holiday, it seemed like a wonderful way to thrill the local folks and bring them on campus at the same time.

From here things started to steamroll! "We can set up our coffee cart with hot cider and throw out some bales of hay and maybe have live Christian music," someone suggested. "We can add a carnival for the kiddies and some cool entertainment with a low-key gospel message for adults," another chimed in.

At this writing, the ground is being cleared for the first-ever Kauai Christian Fellowship Hawaiian Pumpkin Patch and Fall Fun Faire. All because someone looking at an unused lot thought it might look nicer with some pumpkins on it.

This kind of thing is like throwing raw meat to creative types, so make sure that you attempt to implement at least some of their ideas. That's why we gave permission for one of our wildly creative Sunday school teachers to cut holes in the drywall of his classroom and do some imaginative construction. If you are in fourth or fifth grade and stumble into this classroom, you will be astonished to find trap doors, walls that can expand into whole new rooms, a floor laid out in game board patterns, and three-dimensional teaching tools alive with audio and visual sparkle. We have a hard time getting the kids to leave the class when things are over.

So what does this status quo busting get you? An edgy, God-glorifying wildness, a right-side-up church. It often gets better results than whatever you're currently doing. It's fun, stimulating, challenging, stretching, and revitalizing.

And who knows, maybe you will have the privilege of hearing what I heard from a member of our faith community after a worship gathering not too long ago: "You guys are crazy!!! But I love it!"

CHAPTER 3

Rats, Moles, Badgers, and a Toad

A "Classic" Leadership Model

Our leadership team had its dawn patrol meeting today, as it does every Tuesday. At 6:00 AM we gather together—bleary eyed, unshaven, and clutching hot cups of Christian crack from Starbucks—to wrestle with making all the wise and profound decisions that will keep the church from running off the rails. We wrapped up early so we could race our new church go-carts around in the muck and do donuts on the gravel parking lot.

It had rained hard during the evening so we got a bit filthy. Anyone having church business today would probably wonder about the mud-specked fashion being sported by the staff.

This seems to me to be appropriate behavior for leaders. We Christian leaders often take ourselves too seriously. We think that we are or must be, spiritually speaking, the "great and powerful wizard of Oz" when in reality we are simple, little men desperately pulling levers behind the curtain of our profession hoping to somehow whiz-bang everyone else.

How many of us use our theological training so that we can toss around terms like "soteriology" and con others into thinking that we somehow have an insider's view of spirituality? Does it give us the illusion of power to be able to bat around words that 95 percent of our flock have no clue how to define?

Sometimes the language we use as Christian leaders becomes mere lingo, or worse, spiritual gobbledygook. Or to steal from Tolkien, we assume the magic mantle of Gandalf but we are really halflings who have been assigned to carry power we dare not claim for ourselves.

It's important to me that people understand that we who devote all of our time to the work of the church are not magic.

On a puddle-jumping flight I happened to sit near a family coming back from a vacation. The kids attend our church but their parents do not. Even though this was a short flight, the mother was a ball of nerves. She dug her nails into the seat and grimaced in fear-of-flying angst.

As the flight got underway she leaned over to tell me that her fear was relieved by the fact that I was on board. God wouldn't let the plane crash when one of His VIPs was on it.

Apparently she had mistaken me for a talisman. (A bit of musing on the fate of the prophet Jonah should make anyone traveling with a "man of God" want to run off the plane rather than find solace from his presence there.)

I assured her that while my presence had nothing to do with the safety of the plane, God no doubt had everything under His control.

I have a low-level resentment of the fact that at most every gathering, even among fellow Christians, I am called on to bless the food—as if because I am a pastor I have some tighter connection to the Almighty than does the average hungry saint. Maybe they figure it's what they pay me for. I am always gracious about the request but occasionally I feel like shouting, "Would the person in the room who is the most grateful for food tonight please throw out a prayer of thanksgiving?" . . . 'cause it ain't always me!

I must also admit that my mouth goes dry during some tough situations in which the wise and gentle hand of a pastor is most needed. I have nothing to offer that will soften the blow when a family loses a child or a wife loses a husband of half a century. I can and do hurt with them, and I suppose that is all that is really needed anyway, but I feel as if I should be able to do more.

Most ministers are required to have something to say every Sunday morning: something deep and profound but highly interesting; moving but not sappy; challenging but not terribly uncomfortable; and, of course, biblically sound and insightful. Because most people have no interaction with the pastor during the typical week, this homily is what proves his worth.

Our report card on this one is usually pretty bad. The average minister speaks far too long, with far too much jargon on things far too removed from the daily grind of life. But the pressure is on because a long string of verbal strikeouts is likely to have all but the die-hard folks in the congregation voting with their feet to try another church or sit home and watch something interesting on TV. And when watching TV is more interesting than what God has to say, you know we are in serious trouble.

What I am saying here is that there are a lot of expectations laid upon those of us God has called to help shepherd His flock and, frankly, none of us is up to the job. If the expectations are unreasonable or the bar is too high maybe we never will be. Our ranks are thinned by the weight of those expectations as we burn out or simply become pretenders.

Maybe what we need is to rethink what we are doing and how we are doing it. Perhaps we can help pastors reposition themselves to take fewer hits on the head and come up with more effective and realistic ways for them to do their job.

There are lots of "models" for those trying to figure out what kind of leadership style is the most godly or works best, and far be it from me to add to the confusion by presenting another grid or template to this crowded field. And yet, frankly, I am terrified by some of them.

We have all seen the "Moses model" (where God speaks to the pastor and the pastor tells the church what they are supposed to do) abused and misused by those for whom power is an ego aphrodisiac.

We have seen the frustration a bottom-up church government brings. Some systems are so committee laden that it takes three months to get the funds to purchase an extra roll of toilet paper. (And please submit the report on just why you need that extra roll of TP, in triplicate.)

Then there is the "corporate model" with the pastor as the chief executive and the board acting as the decision makers. But as we are finding out, imitating American businesses may not be altogether compatible for those working with kingdom principles.

Sometimes other models can be found in strange places. So forgive me if this doesn't sound very spiritual, but we found our leadership model in an old Disney cartoon version of a classic tale titled *The Wind in the Willows*. (The book is great too, but most of our staff have too short of attention spans to sit down and read it.)

In Disney's condensed video version, this story features a variety of riverbank creatures locked in a frantic struggle with the sinister weasels for possession of the magnificent Toad Hall estate, overseen by Thaddeus Toad and his friends the Badger, Rat, and Mole. While much of the story seems to swirl around the ADD temperament of Toad and his wild, adventurous spirit that at times endangers everyone connected with Toad Hall, not to mention Toad Hall itself, it is just as much about the unusual collusion between the friends.

Toad is not a far thinker but he is a colorful, endearing, hopelessly optimistic, and cutting-edge character. Without the cooling influence of his friends, he would be just another shooting star, burning quickly and brightly for a moment before crashing into the earth.

Angus MacBadger is a bit of a crank and is constantly concerned about the excesses of Toad. But left in his own world, Badger would turn in on himself and become crotchety and boring. Toad brings adventure to Badger's otherwise dull and small-minded existence.

Mr. Rat is not so nearly a curmudgeon as his friend the Badger, but he is both cautious and reasonable. He too is energized by the antics of the Toad but is also a ready friend of and go-between for both the Toad and Badger.

Moley, a somewhat introverted little character, is an unmovable ally to the Toad while always remaining sympathetic to the pleas of his more cautious friends. One begins to sense that the Mole has deeper insight into the dynamics of the group than any of the other players.

In the end, the Toad needs the cynicism of the Badger, the reasonableness of the Rat, and the quiet loyalty of the Mole as much as they need his loose-cannon personality. The actions of the Toad both enliven and threaten to undermine the community represented by Toad Hall. As the Toad makes new discoveries in the form of a motor car or airplane, it becomes his role to make sure that something maniacal is about to happen at all times! While quickened by the contagious joy of life the Toad injects with his antics, his friends, in their own way, step in to offer their own form of encouragement, chastening, and support to keep the Toad from getting too out of hand while also keeping the weasels at bay.

This seems to me like a pretty good description of a healthy leadership team: friends who genuinely care about each other but who are made of wildly different stuff. The magic is in the tension. An all-Toad environment creates insanity; an all-Badger world creates sterility.

At Kauai Christian Fellowship we have a wide selection of critters prayerfully using our personalities to guide the church. We have rousing debates about every area that affects a church—

from where to spend money to how to handle some of the nut cases God blesses us with. With every issue the moles, rats, badgers, and toads initially head to their individual corners, but with some cajoling and prying of each other out of our comfortable roles we somehow manage to find some common ground—at least usually.

The leadership models that can be explained with a pyramid or flowchart seem a bit suspect to me. I prefer the image of a circle, like ring-around-the-rosy where the one with the most energy drags the others around and when one falls down we all fall down.

I fully understand that there are years of tradition connected with leadership styles in most mainline churches. Even newer church denominations have a prevalent leadership style, which if not dictated is implied. But out here on the ragged edge of church rethink, those traditions don't have a lot of pull. We are rethinking everything that isn't clearly nailed down by Scripture—including how to structure leadership of the church in a culture that has only a fading memory of that organism.

So whenever I am asked about how our church leadership works, I simply hand over a copy of *The Wind in the Willows* video and advise the curious to watch it.

CHAPTER 4

Creature

Missionary to the Trolls

One day we had to sit down and pick some more leaders for our erupting little church. These needed to be men who met the qualities mandated by Scripture, but they also needed to be individuals through whom it was obvious that God was doing something powerful.

I have come to believe that too often, in our frenzy to find the candidates who have the best pedigree or the most sparkling personality to lead our churches, we may overlook some of the best men and women God has designed for the job. So, bypassing the seminaries and those from academic or power-management pools, we headed straight to the happy hunting grounds for leaders frequented by our Lord Himself.

We went down to the sea.

There we found "Creature."

"Creature" (real but generally unknown name: John) had earned the name in high school by being the proud owner of a beat-up wreck of a jalopy upon which he glued cut-out and plastic dinosaurs, farm animals, and soldiers. Dubbed "The Creature Mobile," the rust bucket didn't last too long, but after its demise the nickname was bestowed on the owner.

Creature came from one of those home-life situations too wild and unbelievable to be invented. Raised in a sleepy California beach town, Creature and his siblings had a pair of alcoholics as parents. But unlike the typical alcoholic, this couple would trot along in almost normal fashion for months at a time, holding down normal jobs in their middle-class neighborhood, and then suddenly the duo would go on a prolonged raging bender that would turn life upside down for several weeks until they righted themselves and returned to the ordinary world.

It was during one of those benders that Creature's parents decided to move to Canada. But in their stupor they forgot to inform all of their family. Therefore, when Creature came bouncing home from high school one afternoon he found the house vacated with no forwarding address or note. The boy spent the next few days with friends until his parents sobered up enough to realize that they were missing their youngest son.

Following in the substance-abuse footsteps of his parents, Creature spent most of his young-adult life dealing and ingesting huge quantities and varieties of drugs. After a while they started doing funny things to his mind.

One afternoon in Santa Cruz, during a highly stoned surf session, Creature came to the amazing conclusion that he was John the Baptist. (See, those things your mother told you about drugs *were* true.) Leaving his surfboard behind, Creature set about on a quest to get disciples. But failing to attract followers from the boardwalk, his chemical-addled mind figured out that the best place to find followers would be at a church. And fortunately for him, it was Sunday evening!

Cruising around town until he found a church service in progress, the bold, disheveled young man became every pastor's nightmare. Marching to the front of the church he grabbed the microphone and announced that he was John the Baptist in search of disciples. None were forthcoming during his rant but eventually the police came and escorted him to the local rubber room.

Still in deep mental space, John continued his quest there in state confinement. "I got lots of followers in there," he quips when telling his story. Eventually Creature sobered up and sheepishly admitted that no, he was not John the Baptist. Creature was released a few days later when it became obvious that his mental condition was drug induced.

Soon Creature found himself working as a bellman and chasing waves in the Hawaiian Islands. But someone was chasing Creature, and when the Hound of Heaven finally cornered him, Creature became a "New Creature."

A man with only a perfunctory high school education to his credit, Creature plowed deep into the Scriptures and found that he not only could understand, but in spite of all the abuse he had given his brain cells, he also could retain. In fact, Creature could commit whole books of the Bible to memory!

Affable, hospitable, and friendly, Creature had a whole network of nonChristian friends whom he categorized as "trolls." So Creature set out to be a missionary to the trolls. The Bible studies at Creature's house became known for the unusual variety of local characters who would show up.

Now, the burly Creature had no sheepskin, no formal training, and a colorful past. While he was great leading small-group Bible studies, he wasn't much of a public speaker or an intuitive thinker. But he had the heart of a shepherd, the skills of an evangelist, and an authentic and effective ability to connect with the often overlooked. In addition, with Creature around you would never need a concordance.

So we made him a founding member of the leadership team. He became Pastor Creature. Not quite a rat, mole, badger, or toad, Creature is his own unique breed who came to us with a slew of catchy "Creaturisms"—weird expressions and greetings (such as a jolly "Hey Bunky!")—that in spite of your best efforts you find yourself inserting into your vocabulary. (Boar!)

Over the years I have sat at the feet of or had friendships with some of the brightest lights in contemporary Christendom: authors, academics, intellectuals, pastors, and entertainers. But I have seldom come across anyone as *effective* in his simple, humble way, or anyone whom I think approximates the kind of characters Jesus Himself selected to carry the good news to the world as my friend Creature.

CHAPTER 5

Teaching Them to Talk Dirty

Embracing the Energy of Change

There is a word so dirty that when you say it in church the reaction is immediate, hostile, and horrified. A word that when uttered has cost many a minister his job and has been the catalyst of banishment for other believers. A word so feared that if it must be used, it is couched in euphemisms or coded language.

That dirty word is *change*.

We are creatures of routine, habit, and comfort. Habits and routines bring security, predictability, and gentle knowingness to our often shaky and unpredictable lives. And comfort—oh, my, we saints do love to be comfortable! Thrill me, chill me, but whatever you do, don't make me squirm!

I think it was no less than C. S. Lewis who said, "God is always comforting but never comfortable."

He got that right.

Since Christianity is a faith that demands constant reflection and then change based on that reflection, we had better not get too comfortable. And maybe a good time to practice getting used to change would be when we come together in church.

While the truth that a Christian community holds onto is changeless, the method of imparting that truth, the doorways to the heart of our societies, and the cultural taboos and mores are always in flux. And to be able to communicate God's eternal truths in meaningful and relevant ways, having the ability to quickly adapt and change our means and methods is essential.

You can see the results of churches that have broken the mold and have done some serious rethinking about *how* they will connect with the community they live in. These are the churches that are growing! And likewise you can see the results in churches that have dug in and resisted change or have lost their biblical moorings and drifted with the rest of the culture. They are shrinking in size, increasingly irrelevant, toothless, and powerless. In time all that will be left is a shell of a building that used to house a vibrant church but has been turned into some kind of a funky restaurant.

It is important to remember that virtually every denomination started off with unfettered exuberance propelled by change. Many were on the cutting edge of their day and came into being as a response to the status quo church life that was failing to engage or authentically serve vast slices of the birthing culture. But within each church the tendency to drop anchor and slow down the very vehicle that carries a "new work" to success is inherent. Over a span of time, these mobile, inventive, and fresh approaches become frozen, bureaucratic, and stale. The willingness to change is lost, and paralysis sets in.

All of these realities came crashing down on our little cluster of moles, badgers, rats, and toads as we attempted to hammer out what might be the legacy of this brand spankin' new little church we were about to launch. Then somebody said this: "Let's just make *change* a tradition in our untraditional church!"

Wow! There was a novel concept. But could it be done? And if it could be done how would this indoctrination take place and how would it be received?

We decided to start with our worship gatherings. Since we were fortunate enough to have a gaggle of decent worship leaders and musicians we thought it might be interesting to toss on a new kind of worship band each week, so one would never know quite what would hit the stage each Sunday. Would it be folk-rock worship, country-rock worship, acoustic worship, or ear-splitting, full-tilt rock worship? Would the band members be young, old, or mixed? Would it be led by a few middle school students who knew five songs, three chords, and one beat, or by the pros?

You just never knew, and we weren't telling.

And just who was going to give the message? Well, you never knew that either. We scoured the church for good communicators and offered them a shot at the big time. Credentials didn't matter nearly as much as the heart did. (This is why on some Sunday mornings the message was given by the same guy who was serving drinks at the posh hotel bar later that night.)

Now this approach did play havoc with any messages designed

to be a series, but as far as we could tell it was a bit of a pastoral myth to believe that the congregation was waiting with baited breath for the next installation of the Revelation series.

I was elected to be one of the message givers on Sunday morning. Sometimes I have a whole month off between messages. Funny, the congregation seems to like my stuff better when they don't hear me each week. "Prophets without honor" and all that, I suppose.

We also tinker with the seating from time to time as well as the order of the service from Sunday to Sunday. And you never know when a really big surprise will kick in—such as a whole hula halau rising from their seats within the congregation to do a wonderfully choreographed praise hula as part of a worship song. (A perk that makes up for the high cost of living in Hawaii.)

We especially like to add little touches to keep folks off balance: Fill out a card with your name on it that is collected and distributed for the new owner to use as a daily prayer reminder; find a person you don't know during a time of greeting and make a date to get together for a meal or coffee. Interactive elements occasionally worked into the worship gathering or the message allow for variety, diversity, and a sense of expectation.

One of my favorite Sundays was when we ended by throwing dozens of beach balls into the auditorium and told folks they weren't dismissed until they had batted the ball. (This came on the heels of a couple real *serious* Sundays in a row, and it seemed like we needed to be reminded that for the most part, being a Christian is fun!) I have to admit, this whole mindset makes it pretty enjoyable and interesting even for those of us who are in charge of putting together the program for each Sunday morning.

This off-balance, you-never-know-what-you-are-going-to-get kind of tradition permeates everything we do. So when change happens nobody is surprised, nobody is bothered, nobody is fazed in the slightest. We have taught them to talk "dirty."

But try to give them the same old thing over and over again, and boy will they start to bellyache!

CHAPTER 6

Herding Cats

The Art of Shepherding in the Twenty-first Century

The Bible school I attended in Europe thought it was a good idea to involve the students in some kind of stress-relief program that could also benefit the school. Therefore each Friday was set aside for a workday within the facility or on the massive pastoral estate that surrounded the school.

Students were given the opportunity to sign up for an area of slave labor. There was carpentry—not a choice I would make due to a birth defect that had connected thumbs in the places where fingers should go. There was housecleaning—p l e a s e, some things are even below the dignity, and skill level, of a male college student. There was gardening—a duty that seemed as if it might be rather on the dainty side or could possibly be a euphemism for "yard work," a chore for which as a youngster I had developed a severe allergy. Finally, there was farming.

Yeah! Farming! According to my mother, who was raised on

a South Dakota farm, farming ran in our veins. Even though the only crop I had managed to raise and harvest was a single watermelon that grew where I would spit my seeds, my aspirations were high. Tough, rough, and romantic! I would be a Friday farmer!

We farming hopefuls and posers were assigned to a squat, powerful, pug-faced, no-nonsense professional Irish farmer. His thinly veiled disdain for all of us rookies seeped out of his pores. Eventually he weeded out the fakers from those with some actual farming ability. He then found something innocuous to do for those of us who were merely taking up space on the tractor seat.

We rejects were sent to herd sheep.

Now that was a new adventure for a Southern California beach kid. I figured it was as close to being a cowboy as one could get in wet, foggy Europe. I became Shepherd Rick every Friday! Thus began my limited education in the art of shepherding the flockable, dumb, and defenseless.

The Lord often used sheep as a metaphor for the people He called His own. And of course those who guide them are called *shepherds*, which is what the word *pastor* means. The concept was right out of the context of everyday life of people for centuries. Perhaps Jesus wasn't all that particular about the metaphor, and He just grabbed the sheep example because it was nearest at hand and everyone could relate.

As a one-day-a-week shepherd I found that I had no affinity for the critters. I never called them by name or knew if they had a name. "Here, Stupid" was my universal address. We never bonded. I was strictly a sheep security guard, watching my assigned flock in total boredom, waiting in vain for some excitement in the shape of the big bad wolf or a sheep-stealing varmint to arrive.

One thing I did notice about sheep is that they had a tendency to stick together.

If you could get two, three, or four going in the right direction, most of the rest would follow along, leaving the job to round up the few moronic strays—something that could be done with a fair bit of ease.

Given the rather docile, herd mentality of the church suggested by the sheep metaphor, I have often thought how different shepherding is when it comes to the typical rank-and-file characters that stumble into the church today. These folks are anything but sheep. Many are skeptical, highly independent, hesitant, and downright skittish.

More like cats than sheep.

In fact, it seems to me that being a shepherd in this era is like trying to herd cats. We are no longer "pastors" as in the idea of shepherds. Rather, we are Cat Herders. (Sorry, I'm not sure what the Greek term for this would be.) You can get a few cats moving in the direction you are guiding, but most of them peel off on their own adventures or give you that "don't expect much from me, buster" look that cats do so well.

Cats come and go at will. They think nothing of taking off for a while and doing their own thing before deciding to again grace the family with their presence.

This isn't the docile, willing-to-follow group of saints from yesteryear. These are autonomous, self-willed, and sometimes cantankerous believers who seem to view the church as the spiritual equivalent of a department store: a place where you can pick and choose whatever fits you.

Actually, you don't herd cats. You attract them. You win the right to their devotion.

Give a cat enough bowls of milk, diversion, and careful petting, and sooner or later that independent feline comes and jumps in your lap, plays with you without breaking your skin with its teeth—or even goes so far as to give you the lick of love.

I have to admit that cat herding can be a bit frustrating. The floating, low commitment level of many of the people entering the community of faith is a terrible commentary of what our culture has produced. It plays havoc with decency and order. And those with feline tendencies will find that God is out to change them in a serious way. The frustration can be doubled when you add a bunch of feral cats into the mix.

I've come to the conclusion that assuming the church is full of people waiting eagerly to be guided toward godliness is a load of crock. This is the desire of some, to be sure, but the vast majority of folks are a complicated tangle of spiritual and carnal desires, hurt, insecurity, ignorance, misconstrued priorities, and pride. Yet sometimes they soar in their ability to hone in on the heart of God. They don't much like being preached at, but they really enjoy being loved, encouraged, challenged, and affirmed. They turn their noses up at church activities and offerings that don't tempt their palates but gang up around things that do.

Sometimes we have had to learn the hard way about herding our cats. We have misread or presumed upon our congregation and launched some Bible study or church ministry that bombed.

If we were leading sheep it would be easy to get bitter and start talking to ourselves in the "I work hard to give these ungrateful folks what they need to grow spiritually and they can't even commit to one evening a week to attend a home Bible study" mode. But when we came to realize that we were leading cats, we just figured that we would have to rethink the whole way of doing church.

Our leadership team is constantly surprised at what our folks go for. For example, when we realized that many were turning their noses up at the idea of a long-term weekly Bible study (too much commitment required), we decided to take a few months' worth of teaching and cram it into one Saturday disguised as a One Day Bible School, complete with tuition, diplomas, a wide offering of electives, recess, and cafeteria lunch. The cats came charging out for that offering and meowed for more!

But what attracts them is not always consistent, like the cat who gets bored with the same old kitty kibble and leaves the dish full to go find a bird or a mouse. These people are fluid. And that part of their nature really keeps us on our toes.

So we experiment. A lot. If something takes off we jump on it and ride it until it runs out of gas, then go looking for the next thing to hop on. This year we did away with our typical weekend men's retreat and launched a "floating" men's retreat by renting a large beach house for a whole week in front of one of the best surf spots on the island. The only thing organized was the barbecue feast at dusk and the Bible study that followed. Men were encouraged to invite other surfers they met in the water to dine with us. People could join us for one night or join us every night, stay over or head home; it didn't matter. A staff member was at the house 24/7 and the fridge was always full. The ultimate in hang-loose retreat planning.

Wow! Did that idea work! There is a caterwauling demand for a rerun next year.

We're never sure what's going to work to bring folks of the feline persuasion home. So we just smile and put out the bowls of milk. And, hopefully, we'll keep attracting more cats to the herd.

CHAPTER 7

Full-Size Candy Bars

Being Spooky for the Kingdom

I think it is the solemn duty of all pastors to pass out full-size candy bars on Halloween.

Yes, I know that for many Christian folk this holiday is one born out of the depths of hell, and we must protect our children from it by wearing our costumes and passing out our candy in the safe confines of the church building. But in spite of the best efforts of our alarmists, it seems nobody has gotten the message about the evils of Halloween to the droves of grade school vampires, Spider-men, fairies, and witches who, with bulging pillowcase in hand, tromp up our porch steps on the thirty-first of October.

I live in an actual neighborhood. Unlike some anonymous and sterile suburbs, ours is an old-fashioned kind of place where people actually are acquainted with each other and give a wave when they drive by. Our children co-mingle for water balloon fights, birthday parties, and bicycle expeditions to the end of the block.

Most everyone around knows that I am a professional religious guy—a pastor, reverend, priest, voodoo cult leader, or something like that. Out here in the neighborhood I'm never asked to give a message—I am the message. My integrity and authenticity are judged in a different way here than church folks judge it.

So if I stop and jump out of my car to retrieve a neighbor's empty errant trash can from the street where it's been blown on trash day, I give a message. If my kids trudge off to the same public school as the rest of the kids, I give a message. If at school I volunteer to chaperone field trips or be one of the guest classroom speakers on "Career Day," I give a message.

We Christians give messages all the time. Sometimes they are not very good ones.

The family next door always made Halloween a goofy, fun, quasi-spooky time by turning their front yard into a maze of tombstones, spider webs, black lights, blazing jack-o'-lanterns complete with cheesy-creepy sound-effects CDs. Their efforts were guaranteed to terrify any kid under the age of three. For everyone else the haunted house decor just provided a bit of seasonal excitement and joy.

Then the mom became a Christian, and all fun ceased.

Her kids, to their horror, were forbidden to decorate or go trick-or-treating. Instead, they were forced to suit up as Bible characters and be dragged off to a Harvest Party instead. The house that had once been festive and ablaze with creepy fun would remain dark and abandoned on Halloween. The rest of the neighborhood didn't really know what had happened, only that the woman had "gotten religion." And the results were no fun. Her family would no longer play the game everyone had so enjoyed.

The terrible thing about this turn of events was that we (my newly converted neighbor and I) were supposed to be on the same side of all the issues—and we were not. The alarm inside me was starting to go off. I recalled that when I was a kid roaming the neighborhood on Halloween, there was a sense of judging the heart of the occupants by their willingness to play the game well. If the wife answered the door she would coo about the cute pirates (Cute pirates? Who ever heard of a cute pirate?). If the man answered the door he would mumble something, dole out the demanded bribe, and get back to his sports program.

This was the norm. But among those playing the game there was always someone in the territory (all kids have a territory; it enlarges a bit as they get older but it still remains their domain) who really loved kids. Someone who understood and gave out the currency of a kid's Halloween kingdom: fun and loot. These were the folks who did one of two things: decorated their homes in a cool, creepy way, or gave out full-size candy bars rather than the little cheapies most people gave. Sometimes, on a rare occasion, they did both things.

Now I've got to tell you: kids remember. They remember things for a long time. They spread the word about those who are benevolent to the values of kid-dom. They hold those households in honor. Months after Halloween my childhood gang would bike past a home where full-size Snickers bars had been handed out and someone would say in hushed reverence, "That's the house where they gave out big candy bars." And everyone would smile and nod with greedy approval.

So I decided that our family would be that house now that the new Christian lady on the block had put the kabash on Halloween. I wanted kids passing by in the school bus weeks after Halloween to point to our home and say, "Those guys gave out full-size candy bars." I want the goodwill and praise of children—and their pagan parents. I want them to think of us as fun. (We are.) I want, if even in a backhanded way, to give them the message that God is generous and fun as well.

To give our Halloween presentation a little more finesse, I replaced the outdoor lights with black lights and hid a fog machine under the stair landing with the controls running clandestine into the house. The squeal of delight that came from kids traversing the driveway was part of the payoff. The widened eyes as I held out a cauldron of full-size candy bars was another return on my investment.

But it is knowing that with mere candy bars I may be paving the road for future willingness on the part of these kids and their families to listen to and experience the reality of Jesus that really gets me excited.

Because kids do remember.

CHAPTER 8

And Then Jesus Danced

Caring for the "Least of These"

It's funny how something we think we have lost is often right in front of our eyes—or in the case of sunglasses, right on top of our head.

I find I have this amazing knack, when absorbed in seeking what is lost, to never be able to find it—and when not looking for it at all, to have it drop in my lap.

I kick myself quite often for not being very alert to things that really can make a difference that are right there out in the open. Sometimes, though, I get lucky, and one of those "ah-ha" moments pops up just to see what I will do with it. In fact, some of those opportunities have turned into life-changing events.

At our local high school the Christian kids pretty much do what you would expect Christian kids to do at any secular school around the country. At the beginning of the school year they try to muster up some troops to gather around the flagpole before school in a show of solidarity and prayer. They exercise their constitutional right of freedom of speech to form a Christian club on campus and try, successfully or unsuccessfully, to get all the Christian kids to attend one day a week during lunchtime. Sometimes they even pull off a cloak-and-dagger move and sneak some Christian muscle guy on campus to wow the kids by blowing up hot water bottles until they explode, or by breaking bricks with his head. Sometimes I even come on campus at lunchtime to give a short devotional pep talk.

It's nice. Mildly exciting and occasionally life altering. But most of these things actually don't accomplish much, and some are merely "ornamental" in nature. I've noticed that ornamentation rather than penetration seems to be a common trait of a lot of Christian activity.

It was after one of these lunchtime campus Bible study gatherings that one of those rare "ah-ha" moments came. A small cluster of us were standing outside in the courtyard waiting for the end-of-lunch bell to ring. The banter of the moment was all about one of the crowning school events of the year: the Winter Ball. Who was taking whom, what they were wearing, what they were driving, and so on. You know, the little big deals that high school is made of.

While the kids were babbling, I caught a glimpse of a group of students being rolled and guided down a distant walkway. They were the special education kids. They each had mild to somewhat severe mental challenges. If the truth be told, they were the lepers of the school. Someone in a district office had decided that these kids should be "mainstreamed," and therefore they attended high school with the rest of the "normal" kids.

I should say they "sort of" attended school with the rest of the kids. They were on the same campus but occupied separate classroom spaces, and they were soundly ignored by their peers and virtually absent from participation in student activities. I think they'd be among what Jesus referred to as "the least of these" to whom He compared Himself.

"Too bad those kids will never go to a Winter Ball," I thought out loud to one of the kids idling about.

It was as if a bolt of lightning had suddenly struck. Scales fell from eyes and the same thought raced through a few minds . . . *what if?*

What if? became Why not? And before too long plans were rolling for something that had never been done at the school: a Winter Ball for special ed kids. This event, however, would not be like the Special Olympics where the handicapped are in the field and the regular folks are cheering them on. No, this ball would be for both groups of kids, tossed together for a night to remember.

The stunned administration had to be assured the Christian students weren't joking. So the kids got busy organizing themselves into committees to arrange for music, decor, and refreshments. As the time for the Special Winter Ball approached, the kids had secured a live rock band (something not even the mainstream Winter Ball had been able to procure), cookies were being baked, posters made, and one big kid was conned into being "Santa" and given a costume and pillowcase full of candy.

I still have the video of the first time this event occurred, and I have to admit to getting a little misty every time I watch it. It shows dozens of high school kids quietly waiting in a large decorated school cafeteria. Suddenly the special ed kids are wheeled or stumble awkwardly through the doors. And there goes up such a cheer and applause from their fellow students that the recipients nearly freeze in their steps.

Soon the band kicks in and the kids from the Christian club (and others they have drafted) race toward these castaways and manage to drag them on to the dance floor where they proceed to shake, groove, and wiggle with their flailing, spastic partners. For virtually all of these handicapped kids it was their first time dancing with a member of the opposite sex.

When the party wound down and the guests of honor left, exhausted, sweaty, and still licking at the chocolate chip cookie remnants smeared across their lips, a wave of satisfaction spread throughout the kids in the Christian club. They had touched something, sensed something, and experienced something unexpected and delicious. Something that their own Winter Ball with its glitz and glamour couldn't match.

They had danced with Jesus. They had raced around the room pushing His wheelchair. They had baked Him cookies and fed Him 7-Up-laced punch.

> "I was hungry and you fed me,
> I was thirsty and you gave me a drink,
> I was homeless and you gave me a room,
> I was shivering and you gave me clothes,
> I was sick and you stopped to visit,
> I was in prison and you came to me."

... "Master, what are you talking about? When did we ever see you hungry and feed you, thirsty and give you a drink? And when did we ever see you sick or in prison and come to you?" ...

"I'm telling the solemn truth: Whenever you did one of these things to someone overlooked or ignored, that was me—you did it to me."

(Matthew 25:35-40, MSG)

While it is a nice thing to call down the blessings of God around the flagpole each fall, and it is wonderful to meet as a Christian club, I somehow think that Jesus would rather be dancing.

CHAPTER 9

A Whuppin'

Opening Wide the Doors to God's House

It doesn't take too much imagination to hear the dialogue between some of the "Jesus boys" that could have sprouted up around a smoky campfire in the boondocks outside Jerusalem 2,000 years ago.

"Hey, Andrew, whut's that thing the Master's fiddlin' with?"

"Can't you see, Thaddeus? It's cord."

"Yeah, but why's he tyin' up the ends in those tight little knots? Whut's he tryin' to make?"

"I dunno . . . kinda looks like a whip of some kind."

"Uh, hey, Andrew, why don't you ask him what he's making?"

"You're the one who wants to know, Thad. You ask him."

Brief silence.

"Uh, um . . . Master, is that a whip you're a makin'?"

"Yep."

More silence. Then whispers.

"Andrew, Jesus said he's makin' a whip. What do you think it's for?"

"Probably to give someone a whuppin'."

"Man, I wonder who's gonna get it."

"Maybe he's finally gonna give some of those highway-robbing, traitorous, rotten, God-forsaken tax collectors what they deserve. (Uh, no offense, Matthew.)"

"Ooh, maybe we'll catch a Roman soldier wandering around all by himself in the middle of the night. Woo-hoo! Simon the Zealot would love to get in on that action!"

"Wonder if Jesus plans to finally clean up the red-light district?"

"What? And put yer mother outa work?"

"Shut your face, you jerk!"

"Hold up! I'm just messin' with you, Andrew."

"So why don't you ask him, Thaddeus? Ask him what he's gonna do with that whip he's making."

"Okay, I will! . . . Er, Lord, are you making that thing so you can whup people?"

"Yep."

(Aside) "Holy cats! Andrew, we *are* gonna whup people! . . . "Lord, where's we gonna go to whup people?"

"Church, Thaddeus. We're gonna go to church and whup some people."

Long silence.

(Whispered) "Well, Andrew, you can't ever say hangin' out with the Master is boring."

Most of us know the end of this story. Jesus went on a rampage inside the temple, driving out those who had turned a place of worship into a bazaar.

Now it wasn't the selling of animals and grain to be used in the temple sacrifice that riled Jesus up. In fact, due to the long distances people traveled to come to the temple, these services were both important and necessary. It was that these merchants had, with the approval of the temple authorities, set up their wares in the outer courtyard of the temple itself. And it was in this courtyard *only* that women, children, and any believer in God of non-Jewish origin was allowed to fulfill their temple duties. Jewish-born *men*, on the other hand, could escape the noise, smells, filth, and confusion by stepping into the second enclosure reserved for them. There they could worship God without the distractions inflicted upon the lesser mortals. In short, it was the fact that this confusing mess made worship difficult for those who were considered the "lesser" part of Jewish society that puts Jesus taking a whip in hand into context.

We undoubtedly can do a lot of things that annoy God, but if you want to get a taste of good old-fashioned divine vengeance, just start throwing stumbling blocks in front of people, especially the young or lesser ones who want to worship Him.

There was an era (a long time ago) when I resembled a surf-stoked Viking invader, resplendent with shoulder-length blond hair and a full reddish beard. But in spite of my wild-man grooming, I had committed my life to following, serving, and worshiping Jesus. I remember showing up for church one Sunday morning and finding a board member positioned at the entrance door, smilingly passing out small printed business cards. He looked at me gleefully as he handed me a card.

I took a seat and read the card. Printed neatly on a profession-ally made business card were these words in the best King James English: *Doth not even nature itself teach you, that, if a man have long hair, it is a shame unto him? 1 Corinthians 11:14.*

A wave of consternation came over me. It had nothing to do with the theology of the verse printed on the card but every-thing to do with the message of the card and the heart and motive behind it.

Now, I have to admit that I didn't feel much like joining the church in worship that morning. And I didn't feel particularly loved, wanted, or cared for. Frankly, I wanted nothing more to do with that church or anyone in it—which was really a lousy feeling considering that I was employed as their middle school youth pastor.

I didn't lose faith but I lost heart.

Fast forwarding a few decades I found myself part of a church-planting team. Now *we* had to make decisions that would affect the ease in which people would be drawn to worship God. Would we, by foolishness or by a darker motive (such as pandering to those who would be most likely to throw down bucks), create an environment that excluded or alienated people trying, some for the first time, to connect with spiritual things?

We asked ourselves hard questions about who we wanted to make sure not to keep on the other side of our church doors. To whom did we want to erect the fewest barriers so those on the "outside" might be drawn into worship? Our answer? Tenth-grade boys. Those very creatures who typically find a worship service a drudgery, who don't raise their voice to sing because they don't much like the music and don't much like the sound of their own voice, those young men who doodle on the bulletin in the back of the church, those teens who can't relate to much being said on a Sunday but who are destined in a few years to take the helm of the church. Yes! We would *intentionally* target these most unlikely worshipers as we selected the song set or crafted a message.

When we launched the church, it was with the conviction that there are lots and lots of churches designed to connect with those on the inside track of Christianity. We would choose to spend our time in those "outer courts," helping remove the barriers that had kept those folks from being able to freely worship and understand.

The result? As it turned out, there were an awful lot of adults who seemed to be energized and animated by the "youthfulness" of our aim. But they have learned that if they plan on getting a seat in the front two rows they had better get to church early in order to beat all the kids.

It's loud, vigorous, and colorful at Kauai Christian Fellowship on Sunday mornings. The Lord is there—and He isn't giving whuppings.

CHAPTER 10

The Inner Sanctum

Pride of Ownership

It was well before dawn on an Easter Sunday, back near the beginning of time . . . somewhere around the mid-seventies. I was a green youth pastor who had come to work in a church that had a set of well-founded traditions of which the *Official All Church Easter Morning Pancake Breakfast Youth Fundraiser* was one. The kids were to act as waiters while the adult sponsors did the food prep. Sounds simple enough: Sling out some hotcakes and a few sausages to help with the arteries and make a load of bucks for the kids.

What I hadn't reckoned on was the inner sanctum.

Like most church facilities, this one in California had a standard kitchen with a few mismatched implements, dinged up frying pans, a microwave, and a coffee pot. Naturally not just anyone could stroll into the kitchen and whip up lunch. One had to have the key and to have been knighted worthy of entrance by the gods of the kitchen. In this case, the "gods" were the ladies in charge of the women's ministry.

At the rear of the kitchen was a heavily padlocked door that I had only glimpsed as I had passed the kitchen. (Being too new and untested I was not considered by the kitchen gods to be worthy of a key.) This door led to the holy of holies of the church building, the place where the *good* skillets and the *good* dishes resided. Inside this inner sanctum were a half dozen cupboards, each padlocked against intruders. Only the kitchen gods possessed a set of keys to the holy of holies and the secrets padlocked in their cupboards.

Now, back to early Easter morning. The chef for this event was my right-hand staff assistant Bob McDonald. Short, jolly, and rotund, Bob in real life was actually a quick-order chef, but because he had thrown his lot in with the youth department he never made the list of those worthy to possess a key to the inner sanctum. Due to the hideous hour that the breakfast food had to be prepped, Bob was promised by the kitchen gods that a set of keys to the sacred interior would be on the counter just inside the commoner's kitchen.

It was four o'clock in the morning when Bob and I waded into the dark kitchen loaded down with supplies. I heard him mumble something (which sounded to be a bit more than a minced curse) under his breath.

The key was missing.

Sweat broke out on Bob's forehead. Crimson rose on his neck. He began to say some very, very unpleasant things about the kitchen gods.

"Maybe we should call, wake them up, and have them bring us a key," I suggested.

"No time for that!" roared Bob as he stormed out of the kitchen.

A few moments later Bob returned with furrowed brow, sweating, red faced, a crowbar in hand. This was a clear portend of trouble.

Bob said nothing to me. He simply marched to the door of the holy of holies and with a mighty snap destroyed the cheap lock and hasp that held us at bay. The door rolled open. Bob then burst into the bowels of this most sacred place and one by one ripped the hasps off the cupboard doors. With each yank of the crowbar and clatter of the hardware on the counter I could hear his voice calling down hellfire on the kitchen gods.

As they say in Hawaii, we were about to be in "deep kimchee."

The good news is that feeding the masses went off without a hitch and right on schedule. The bad news is that the kitchen gods didn't appreciate Bob's redecoration of the inner sanctum and banished both of us from entry into any kitchen facilities at all, for eternity.

Many years have passed since "the incident" as a fledgling youth pastor at Bob's side. But when Kauai Christian Fellowship was in the final stages of our building program, the memory came back to haunt me. For a number of years we had squeezed our growing congregation into inadequate rented facilities in a small office complex. Finally, after much sacrifice and many small and large miracles, six acres of land had been purchased and a wonderfully huge new building was nearing completion.

It was as the final coat of paint was drying and finish carpentry work was taking place that I began to hear the voices of those staking out a claim. The music guys were intent on putting their gear in a special room under their own set of locks and keys to keep all those grubby paws away from their stuff. The women were moving hard toward kitchen domination. The process of picking gods and goddesses was building up steam.

We were quickly going down the path that so many other churches had gone down before unless something was done to stop it. It didn't take much imagination to see that soon a back-stooping wad of keys would be needed just to maneuver from one end of the campus to another and anyone wanting access to set up their space would encounter endless bureaucracy with accompanying security clearances set up for control of those keys.

It is the natural drift for churches to create a fortress, to erect barriers of safety, walls and fences of protection for all those terrible things that just "might" happen if the wrong person gets in. We church folks worry a lot about what "might" go wrong. We fret about what "might" happen if some malevolent character slips into our Sunday school classroom, gets his hands on the copy machine, or has access to the supply cupboard. So to protect ourselves from any "mights" that could occur, we load ourselves down with official procedure, busy work, and padlocks—safety measures that usually inhibit only those who are law-abiding citizens in the first place but seldom keep out those intent on harm—or those frustrated workers swinging a crowbar in the holy of holies.

I asked myself what "might" happen if we didn't behave like a typical church. What might happen if we operated out of faith and trust in our people rather than paranoia and fear? What might happen if we didn't let bureaucracy and red tape get a foothold? What might happen if we keyed *all* the doors to open with the same key? And what might happen if we ruined the plans of all those vying for the position of god or goddess and gave *every* family in the church a key?

I could see there could be some risk, but I could also imagine that we may have a wild harvest of benefit as well. What kind of ownership, stewardship, gratitude, responsibility, and industry might result if *all of us* were entrusted with a key that opened any door in the new building that we all had worked and sacrificed so much to create? What kind of empowering might result from knowing that you can get access to the materials, tools, and even cleaning supplies that you need to do whatever ministry God has called you to? Sure, someone could pull up to the pantry and load up his trunk with a year's supply of toilet paper, but how likely was that? I wagered what was more likely was that the bathroom would never run out of toilet paper because everyone would be able to get into the closet that held it!

At our next leadership meeting I proposed this crazy concept. The moles and badgers in the group swallowed hard, but to their credit they decided that the good "mights" outweighed the bad "mights."

Just before our new church opened in October of 2002 a letter was sent to every active family. The letter commended our family of faith for a job well done and challenged them to use this sparkling new campus to advance God's kingdom with care and responsibility.

In the middle of each letter was a single, shiny key to the church.

It opens *every* door in the building to this day.

And while we have had a few bumps along the way (just how did those high school kids get a copy of the key anyhow?), the place is a beehive of activity day and night with people doing the very things that we had hoped they would do.

I think people in the real estate business call it "pride of ownership."

CHAPTER 11

What Disneyland Can Teach Us

Improving First Impressions

Disneyland wrote the book on first impressions.

The kaleidoscope of sights, the various theme-appropriate sounds that follow you through the park, and the exciting and visually stimulating environment that springs upon you once you pass the turnstiles have been carefully orchestrated.

My dad helped build the original Disneyland in Anaheim, California. Our family would often go check out the progress of his little tiny corner of the Magic Kingdom. Thus from early in life I have been an incurable Disneyland junky.

Somebody was (and is) doing some hard thinking when it came to designing the "experience" of going to Disneyland. And I find that their hard thinking can actually teach those of us in the church a thing or two. For starters, they understand that the initial encounter a person has with the park sets the tone and mood for the rest of the visit. Within the first twenty steps they want you to say "this is going to be good!" (And within the next ten steps to break out your wallet.) Disneyland goes so far as to have a vat of vanilla cooking over Main Street eateries with its "smells like something good is cooking" message being blown by fans into the street to get those salivary glands going.

Everyone who works in the park is considered part of a vast play or drama with their own given roles, patter, and costumes. They are not employees, they are *cast members*. I like to think of all of us in the church in the same way. We are cast members in a great and ultimate Passion Play, picked by the Author, Producer, and Director of all things to serve well in the role that we have been given. Some of us have been designated as major characters, some as minor characters, some to provide services, be a guide, or create music, and some to run around and clean up everyone else's mess—all at the behest of our Maker.

Those who study church outreach say that the first five minutes make all the difference in the mind of a visitor to any community of faith. It makes no difference how nice and friendly all the saints of our little church are "once you get to know them." If they don't wear that niceness and friendliness on their sleeve and get out of their own comfort zone to interact with newbies, few will stick around long enough to get to know them.

Those of us who have been in churches a long time may have forgotten what a huge step it is for someone new to come and visit, especially if it has been years since they darkened the door of a church. A poor first impression often turns off a visitor for good.

If we are honest, most of us have never walked into a church and within twenty steps said to ourselves, "This is going to be good!" More often we are thinking, "Uh, oh, this looks like it could be weird."

The folks at Disney are students of humanity. They often understand us far better than we do ourselves, and they take steps to preempt our bad behavior or, put another way, "redirect us toward the positive."

For example, someone at Disney did a study on people who are holding a bit of trash or garbage. They found that the average person would hold on to a piece of trash for twenty-seven feet before deciding merely to toss it on the ground or in the bushes. That's why in Disneyland there is a trash container every twenty-seven feet.

They understand what motivates people to buy, to return, and they even know patterns of how people will walk and have used them to help to steer people through the Magic Kingdom efficiently. They saw that people always tended to cut corners so they have no right angles in their sidewalks but only curves.

Those of us who work with people for the sake of the real Kingdom might do well to study the humanity we have been given to work with as well. When vast amounts of my time were spent working with middle school kids, I found it was to the benefit of the lesson I had spent a lot of time working up to arrive at the classroom early and prowl around looking for anything that might be turned into a distracting toy or weapon of annoyance. I would mentally imagine that I was a seventh grader and then creep through the classroom in that mindset looking around for something I could fire at some other mutt or use to annoy Polly.

Once identified, I would collect those things and put them

out of the way. I made it a point to design the room the way *I* wanted it to be in order to best eliminate distractions, direct my students toward the objective at hand, and keep control and order. In my incarnation as a bored and restless seventh grade boy I viewed the room to see what windows I could stare out, what furniture I could play with or draw on, and what I could use as a drum, cymbal, or mode of transportation. Then I removed them or rearranged the room to disarm those things.

When the kids showed up they were not manipulated into good behavior by my previous work, they were simply given a different context in which they could be kids, a context of my choosing, not theirs. In short, I out-thought them.

Ironically, my coworkers would often marvel at the well-controlled, positively fluid nature of this huge slug of middle school humanity—as if it were something miraculous. It was no miracle; it was merely scheming.

Adults, by the way, have their own patterns that we can either understand and cooperate with or ignore to the detriment of the Kingdom. For example, at our church we wanted people to hang out and shoot the breeze after our worship gathering. We found that tossing down the money to build a coffee cart that even Starbucks would envy and lining the escape route to the parking lot with a table full of food turned the exodus into a slow-motion event. Now we have to tell people to go home.

Like a lot of modern churches we decided that using pews for seating limited the potential use of the main meeting room and had a stiff, starched, churchy feel. So we opted for very nice, cushy stackable chairs.

But something still felt wrong. It was attractive, clean, color coordinated, modern—and sterile. It looked and felt like an auditorium, which, I suppose, is okay—but when that visitor, leery of church, comes creeping across our threshold, I don't want them to feel that they have come into an auditorium. I want them to feel like they have come into a home, into a community, into a family gathering.

So we called in our best interior designer and told her to get us a whole stack of loveseats to mingle in with our comfy chairs. We commissioned artists in the congregation to create things of beauty to hang on the walls. Now we think that when people come through the doors, what meets their eye will put them at ease, erase some of those "bad church experience" tapes stored in their memory, and give them a hint that they are in for something *completely different!*

So thank you, Walt, Mickey, and gang for the inspiration and ideas.

Oh, and by the way, we also have positioned a trash can every twenty-seven feet.

CHAPTER 12

A Church Full of Children

Taking Ourselves Less Seriously

I've been thinking that maybe we adult Christian folks take ourselves too seriously. Maybe we need a good romp in the mud.

Across the street from our house is a vacant lot. When the rains come in hard, the kids in the neighborhood tear off their street clothes, hop into grubbies, and head for the vacant lot where they stomp, roll, and slide through mud puddles. Even through the sound of pelting rain you can hear their screams of delight as they add one more layer of dirt to their bodies.

When you are a kid, getting filthy is fun. Smearing yourself from head to foot is fun! I sometimes watch them through the window, and it sure looks like fun.

But I am an adult. And I am in a serious profession. I have eternal things to think about. I have Bible studies to create, Greek root words to explore, and important phone calls to make.

The guys around Jesus were serious too.

There were healings to be conducted, mass feedings to orchestrate, Pharisees and Sadducees to worry about on top of growing crowd-control problems. There were money situations too. There was food and lodging for a quickly multiplying group of disciples and camp followers.

So when the kids showed up, security barred them. Annoying, immature parasites. "Hey! You kids buzz off!" some staff person probably hollered.

And of course, being the Jesus we think we know but who keeps delivering curve balls, He scolds His handlers, ignores the adults (with probably a few big tithers among them), and invites the kids in to goof off with Him. He even made an object lesson out of them: "The kingdom of God belongs to such as these" (Luke 18:16).

I have come to feel that the comment that often gets tossed my way—"You're nothing but a big kid!"—is perhaps one of the greatest compliments of my career. Yes! I certainly am! And as long as I and the rest of the big kids around here have anything to say about it, we will continue to end some church services by blowing confetti all over the place, having staff meetings for the sole purpose of laughing our heads off at some of our more staid members trying to play body charades.

We will continue to use quotes from *Monty Python and the Holy Grail* in messages, substitute silly pictures in the church photo phone book to tweak long-time members, put plastic centipedes throughout the church office to playfully torment our centipede-paranoid office manager, and play air-soft in the main meeting room.

We will continue to use the childlike possibilities that come with the word "maybe" as we consider things of the Kingdom.

Maybe we need to work less on the nuances of theology and more on our imagination. Maybe we need to have fewer meetings and more play time with each other. Maybe we ought to believe that each of us could actually be what we dream—and maybe we should encourage and believe in each other's dreams. Maybe we should start by encouraging our adult people to dream.

Maybe those of us who think we know so much ought to cast ourselves in the likeness of children who know they know little but are eager to learn more. (This would bring a whole new dimension to a lot of those prickly theological debates grownups love to engage in.)

Maybe we should admit that, like kids clomping around in adult shoes and dragging behind clothes commandeered from the parent's closet, we are *all* really just dressing up and playing pretend much of the time. Especially when it comes to being like Christ.

Maybe we should pass out bubble gum on one Sunday morning and tell our congregation that no one is free to leave until he or she blows a bubble.

Maybe we ought to mandate that our leadership team goes away on a play vacation with each other (no discussing church stuff allowed) paid for by the church. I bet they would come back more fun to work with.

Maybe more people would find the Christian community more interesting if we were the ones having a wild time instead of cringing at the thought of having a wild time.

Maybe if we were simple, trusting, innocent followers of Jesus our hearts might be alive, adventurous, and playful.

Maybe when we had a disagreement with someone, we could take the way of a child, who is willing to make every day a brand-new day and either forget or forgive the grievance so that the cycle of play isn't disrupted. Such an approach would help marriages and all other interpersonal relationships.

Maybe there would be a lot of really interesting changes if we started to adopt the essential elements of a child.

I could probably think of a lot more and make this chapter powerful and profound. But it's raining. The kids are putting on their grubbies and heading for the vacant lot—and I think I'll change out of my good clothes and go get filthy with them.

CHAPTER 13

The Helmet

Choosing Our Battles

Stuffed, placed, and posted around my office is a strange clutter of personal memorabilia—treasures collected and given over the past thirty-something years in ministry. My small work area has a museum feel that a Victorian would love and a clean desk freak would loathe.

In addition to obligatory computer devices, there are pictures of loved ones; framed pages of old, old Bibles; a realistic looking but hollow plaster foot made for holding pens and scissors; a ceramic plaque featuring the impression of tiny hand imprints from our firstborn; a model of a surfboard-laden "Woodie" crowding an already crowded shelf; an original storyboard production drawing from Disney's *Snow White*; . . . and a World War II German helmet that peeks over from the top of my bookcase.

The helmet has a lethal legacy and, considering the rest of the items of honor and whimsy that decorate my workspace, seems at first glance to be a jarring chord of evil thrown into a world of love and light.

And that it is. But I keep it nearby for a purpose. It serves as a warning and a reminder for me.

The helmet was dug from the permafrost in Russia years after the war by family members of my brother's Russian wife. Part of the steel pot is discolored and rusting and part still has the green-grey paint of the German Wehrmacht on it. The leather interior has long rotted away. But inside the lip of the helmet, still clear after war, weather, and more than a half century, is a hand-printed name, written in small, neat white letters: *Stern*.

Sometimes I think about Stern. Who was he? Where was his home? How old was he when he strapped on that helmet and went to fight for Hitler, the Nazi Party, and the fatherland? What became of him? Is his lost helmet a portent of a lost life? Did he suffer and freeze on those desolate Russian fields or did he just cast off his helmet in a mad dash for safety? Did he believe in what he was fighting for or was he a reluctant soldier? Is this helmet the only remnant of a young life, which vanished during the brutal Russian winter, or did Mr. Stern make it back to Germany and settle down with a plump fraulein and enjoy family and peace?

Of what purpose was the life of this soldier Stern? Did the world change for better or worse, or did it change at all because of his life? Or was the life of Stern simply wasted, along with the energy, imagination, resources, and spirit of millions of other men who found themselves fighting, suffering, and dying for something that would never be realized?

Most of all, I wonder if Stern realized that he was fighting for a lost cause. I wonder if he figured out that the flower of his youth was being sacrificed for a system that would not only be extinguished from the earth but would be considered the epitome of all that is evil and wrong with what man has done.

So I keep that helmet, with its curling lip peeping down on me as I work, as a reminder and a warning. The reminder is that not many things *really* matter. The "things that really matter" is a pretty short list. It takes discernment and skill to select among the contenders for that worthy position.

The warning is to take care to fight only for those things that are *worth fighting for* and to fight *with caution and care*. The helmet tells me to pick my battles wisely, justly, humbly, and intentionally. It does not dissuade me from fighting. It does not give me hesitation to fight hard, sacrificially, or strategically for what is nonnegotiable. But it does give me a pretty strict context for that fight. I have learned much from what soldier Stern left behind in frozen Russia.

I am not convinced that the Christian church has done very well in understanding what matters and picking her battles wisely. We divide over issues that on the whole are mere mosquito bites. We play the game of spiritual one-upmanship as if the things we are passionate about are the central point of our faith. We demean our opponents with statements or pronouncements such as "According to *my* Bible . . ." (which must mean that either your Bible is a misprint or you are such a moron that you can't read what it clearly says) or "We declare the *full* gospel" (which implies that your gospel is only half full), "We take the Word of God *seriously*" (which supposes that you don't), "We are *free* in the Spirit" (which insinuates that you have God's Spirit bound up and crammed in a safe vault somewhere), and so on.

Of course the idea behind these statements is that the one making them is in touch with what God is doing, and the rest of us who don't see it that way or do it the same way are spiritual bozos or posers.

As I peck out these words there are churches and Christians blasting each other as heretical or in serious error for having differing views on end times (pre-trib, post-trib, or mid-trib), predestination (was I selected or did I select?), free will (irresistible choice or one of personal volition), length of creation days (six twenty-four-hour days or six eras), preaching styles (verse by verse or topical), church mission styles (seeker sensitive, traditional, emergent), the gifts of the Holy Spirit, frequency and nature of the Lord's Supper and many, many more items and issues. They come set to do battle with their brothers and sisters in Christ, convinced not only of the correctness of their thinking but of the vital and soul-saving importance of their cause. They believe (as Stern must have) that their particular hobbyhorse is the steed they must ride into battle.

Now please don't think that this is a plea for some sticky sweet ecumenicalism that sings out "all you need is love" and binds us together with a group hug. No, I think it is fine and fair to have differing opinions on many of the issues that have come to divide us. I welcome frank, gritty discussions, debates, and solid biblical inquiry on touchy subjects. I even feel that it is appropriate for communities of faith to consider their distinctions as at least part of the glue that holds them together.

For instance, I don't really expect that those who favor various *styles* of worship are going to be attractive or desirable to each other. I can't imagine that the people who draw in a deep breath of holiness from the lines of an old hymn or the soaring notes of the pipe organ will get much out of the earsplitting bass notes and rocking rhythm of our black T-shirt clad worship band. I don't even expect that those folks will easily appreciate it as a valid form of worship. They may have deep suspicions that we have sold out to MTV. And I certainly do not expect them to join our faith gathering.

But neither do I expect them to do battle with us nor would I want to battle with them. Time will tell whether we, they, or both of us and our worship styles are merely a small insignificant thread in the fabric of the Christian faith.

I must admit that I am still struggling through what to fight about and what to just ignore. I have a pit bull residing deep inside of me that begs to be released when the raw meat of a dumb idea or eye-rolling, new spiritual fad is dangled in front of me. And I know that there is a place for theological watchdogs and putting various teachings to the test. There are clearly ditches on both sides of the road.

I do know that I care much less about some of the issues that animated me twenty years ago, ten years ago, or five years ago. I am also sure of much less now than I was decades ago, but at the same time I am far more sure, far more confident, and far more committed to some ideas now than I have ever been.

And when I stand back and look at those things that have become solid ground for me, I find myself in a company of characters both ancient and modern who, in spite of our differences of opinion about things on the periphery, also find that we now are strangely excited by the same words and ideas.

Words that begin with:

We believe in one God,
    the Father, the Almighty,
    maker of heaven and earth,
    of all that is, seen and unseen.

Do I hear an "Amen" from that cantankerous old Tolstoy and the depression-ridden Charles Wesley?

We believe in one Lord, Jesus Christ,
    the only Son of God,
    eternally begotten of the Father,
    God from God, Light from Light,
    true God from true God,
    begotten, not made,
    of one Being with the Father.
    Through him all things were made.

Is that a hoot of joy I hear from that skinny priest Francis in Assisi? Did that big German named Luther wipe the beer foam off his lips and grunt hallelujah?

For us and for our salvation
    he came down from heaven:

by the power of the Holy Spirit
he became incarnate from the Virgin Mary,
and was made man.

Is that little Roman Catholic woman they call Mother Teresa jumping up to give the high five to the gouty Baptist fellow named Spurgeon? Is that cheer coming from Frenchy Blaise Pascal or the Yank Dwight Moody . . . or both?

For our sake he was crucified under Pontius Pilate;
he suffered death and was buried.
On the third day he rose again
in accordance with the Scriptures;
he ascended into heaven
and is seated at the right hand of the Father.
He will come again in glory to judge the living and
the dead,
and his kingdom will have no end.

Who are those faces singing the Hallelujah chorus at the sound of these lines? Could it be Calvin, Booth, Augustine, and Clive Staples Lewis?

We believe in the Holy Spirit, the Lord, the giver of life,
who proceeds from the Father and the Son.
With the Father and the Son he is worshiped and
glorified.
He has spoken through the Prophets.

We believe in one holy catholic and apostolic
Church.
We acknowledge one baptism for the forgiveness of
sins.
We look for the resurrection of the dead,
and the life of the world to come. Amen.

Not only do I believe it, I have experienced the power of the
One who died and rose again. I have tasted His love and His
forgiveness. I join with my early church fathers in drawing a line
in the sand about who He is and why He came that cannot be
crossed.

Yes! These are the words that give context to what matters in
life. These are the guidelines that define how we are allowed to
interpret the Scripture, view our Savior, and evaluate the doctrine
and faith of our brothers or sisters.

Is there not more to the faith than is defined by the creeds?
Obviously, yes. But, if at the end of the day, after all my labors are
done, if those I shepherd can at least line their heart's cry, their
choices, their decisions, and the driving principles of their life up
to these simple, ancient proclamations, it will be enough for me.

CHAPTER 14

Crashing Elbows

Blessed Are the Clumsy in Spirit

We call them "droppings."

They are not from rodents but from the vast hordes of kids who have made the church their favorite place to hang out, and in particular, the open-air foyer the favorite place to chew on food and banter.

In their wake are empty soda cans, half-eaten sub sandwiches, crushed plastic cups, used napkins, candy wrappers, deflated bags of chips, and greasy print marks on the walls. (And imagine how bad it would be if we didn't have a trash can every twenty-seven feet!)

Usually the youth staff cleans up most of it. Usually. But sometimes they don't quite catch it all or catch it quickly enough. In this case, those arriving for whatever the next function happens to be must parade through a gauntlet of kid "droppings."

(To be fair to the kids at this point in the narrative, I probably should point out that plenty of other people contribute to the handprints on the wall and empty pizza boxes left on the patio tables. But since the kids do create the lion's share of the mess they get 100 percent of the blame.)

There was probably nobody who was more bugged by the slovenliness of the kids than Gary. Gary is a no-nonsense ex-marine whose discipline and intensity make everything he does glisten with a military spit-and-polish glow. Among other ministries, Gary makes sure that all the coffee addicts on Sunday are well supplied from his sparkling, immaculate coffee cart.

Since Gary's coffee cart is located in the same foyer as the kids' hangout, the potential for a confrontation was ripe. In fact, the kids had already picked up on his frowns of disapproval and intense body language and had christened him with a nickname: Scary Gary. Nerves were being irritated and sooner or later something was going to hit the fan. The opposing sides, the kids with their "I didn't make the mess so don't blame me" attitude and a frustrated, hard-working adult, were moving toward a classic Mexican standoff.

Christians can sure get on each other's nerves. We say things and do things that drive our brothers and sisters nuts. The flake factor among believers seems to be just as high as among the unwashed hordes. The rub is that we *expect* Christian behavior from Christians and it gets the righteous indignation boiling when we get behavior that is less considerate, less honest, less responsible, and less moral from people who name Christ as Lord. Add to that our own personal quirks and mannerisms and it's no wonder some church folks are coming to blows.

Christians who get irritated at other Christians usually handle their frustration in one or more of the following ways:

1. They gripe about it. Of course this griping is never directly to the person who is offending but to any willing ear about the offender. To make sure we are not guilty of slander or gossip we sometimes cloak our discussion as a "prayer concern."

2. They pull up stakes. This usually means getting out of whatever situation or ministry that puts them in proximity of the offender and sometimes means pulling back involvement, monetary support, or even leaving the church altogether.

3. They say nothing but let bitterness take root. As the poison spreads they find themselves having nothing but disdain for the person who has irritated them.

4. They try to checkmate.

Nobody would have blamed Gary if he did any of the above. There was a real problem with at least some of the kids not respecting the property of others and taking responsibility for cleaning up their own mess. The youth staff seemed unable to consistently get the problem under control or to build into the kids those points of respect that somehow parents had not drilled into them.

Finally Gary took action. And what he did astonished every kid who had ever rolled their eyes when they saw Scary Gary coming their way.

Noticing that on weekends the high school students would show up early and stay well past dinner into the evening, Gary decided he would cook a *free* meal for all high school kids every

Friday. It was a stunning idea. Dozens and dozens of kids showed up for Gary's Grinds. Using simple recipes and food bought cheaply on sale, Gary would whip up a meal at least once a week (and more often in summer), thus endearing himself to the hearts and minds of the students.

Gary was no longer Scary Gary. He was Cool Gary. He got to know the whole varied range of kids and they got to know him.

Now did this surprising act of servanthood change the pigsty behavior of the kids? Well, it helped a bit, and certainly it made some kids more concerned about picking up in order to make sure Gary was pleased. In fact, kids became excited when they saw Gary show up as it usually meant food.

But what it really accomplished was to give Gary a better idea of the bizarre dynamics of teen years that allow an otherwise perfectly normal young man to walk right past the mess he made and not see it because of some hormone burst. And it transformed Gary from a scary, ticked off adult to Gary the guy who cares enough about me to feed me dinner.

We Christians will *always* have the tendency to elbow others. This is because we are fallen creatures, this is because we are clumsy in spirit, this is because we are innately careless or oversensitive or just lack complete understanding. It's what we do about our various collisions and intrusions with each other that is important.

The beauty of Gary's solution is reflected in the seldom followed suggestion offered several millenniums ago: "If your enemy is hungry, give him food to eat; if he is thirsty, give him water to drink" (Proverbs 25:21). Gary responded to clumsy fellow believers by doing something loving for those who had offended him. Creative, caring, loving actions seem to have a way of disarming a tense situation. They put a new spin on problems that we would otherwise handle unwisely.

We have decided to make the actions of Gary legendary. They are the standard by which all other responses to annoying Christians are judged.

So what's the rule of thumb to end any Mexican standoff? Fix a wonderful meal and invite the one who is bugging you.

Courtesy of (former) Scary Gary.

CHAPTER 15

A New Language

Talking with Pictures

It's funny what a difference in communication a few centuries can make.

When New England preacher Jonathan Edwards rose up at the pulpit of his Enfield, Connecticut, church Sunday morning, July 8, 1741, the sermon he had written out in longhand lying in front of him would, for many years, be one of the most celebrated pieces of religious literature in the English language. Entitled "Sinners in the Hands of an Angry God," the sermon contained memorable lines such as: *"O sinner! Consider the fearful danger you are in: it is a great furnace of wrath, a wide and bottomless pit, full of the fire of wrath, that you are held over in the hand of that God. You hang by a slender thread, with the flames of divine wrath flashing about it, and ready every moment to singe it, and burn it asunder."*

Now those who heard Reverend Edwards that Sunday morning would have experienced, as described by a witness, a monotone reading of his long sermon, spoken clearly but in a "moderate voice" demonstrating "gravity and solemnity." In giving his presentation the pastor stood virtually ramrod stiff. Those who saw him preach described this lack of physical motion with generosity: "He made but little motion of his head or hands in the desk, but spake so as to discover the motion of his own heart, which tended in the most natural and effectual manner to move and affect others."[1]

There was no object lesson, video, skit, PowerPoint or multimedia presentation—nothing that would keep the attention span of any modern churchgoer. It was merely a long series of well-crafted scary words, spoken softly. And as unlikely as it might seem today, it packed a wallop!

Edward's sermon slammed into his New England countryside congregation; men and women cried for mercy and even grabbed their seats afraid they would slip into hell. The resulting after-shocks saw thousands converted, many with weeping and demonstrative repentance.

Deliver that same sermon, with the same tenor and cadence as Edwards did to any audience today and see what would happen. (Go ahead, I dare you; you can find the whole thing online). The Puritan's famous sermon that penetrated so deeply then would likely drop with a wondrous thud nowadays.

Something has radically changed in the past several hundred years. And that change has rapidly accelerated in the last fifteen years. The change is to a brand-new kind of language—not one of many words, but of images; not of well-thought-out ideas mapped on paper, but of fluid personal experiences and stories delivered in a variety of ways. It is talking in pictures. And like it or not, this talking in pictures is the voice by which concepts are usually most compellingly transmitted today.

After last Sunday's worship gathering, a woman in the congregation called to say thank you. She stumbled around trying to find the right description for what had moved her to pick up the phone. Finally she said, "Here is what I really like: When you guys present a message I can *see* it; I can understand it and actually *picture* it!"

This is not merely a figure of speech but a pretty good reflection of the elements that were combined together that Sunday: a few cool graphics, a couple of short video clips, some dance, rockin' all-electric worship music, and a story-laden message. There were as many images as there were words.

We have become so dependent on using the tools of projected images, video clips, and the like that if the power ever goes out we will be in serious trouble. (Well, maybe not that serious of trouble; we would just have to go unplugged for that service. It would become an adventure while digging out our generators!)

As with missionaries in a foreign land, we would do well to learn, understand, and speak this new language if we are to have any hope of communicating the message of Christ to the culture we live in.

To understand how all this took place, a little history lesson may be helpful. Prior to the Reformation, imagery was the church's primary means of communication. The typical Roman Catholic church was a feast of imagery: from glass renditions of Bible stories in every window, colorful vestry decor, statues, fonts, plays, songs, drama, and the crucified Christ hanging above the altar. Even down to the architectural design, there was intentional storytelling and symbolism worked into every corner of the church building as well as many of the pageants and feast days.

This was by necessity. Most people were illiterate; much of the worship service was in another language, and the Bible was a mystery book available to an elite few who were educated and wealthy enough to afford one. Much of the Christian education was done by meditating on symbols and picture stories rather than reading and hearing.

The timely convergence of Gutenberg's printing press and Martin Luther's bold reform movement revolutionized society. Printed material was suddenly everywhere. A slim book that one week cost pounds by the next week cost pennies. Literacy began to climb. People gathered on street corners to hear the printed word read aloud.

As the Reformation took hold, all of the ancient trappings of the Catholic Church were up for review. Very few remnants of the old system survived the revolution. In these new "protesting" churches the printed Word became the central driving force. Among many of the newly spawned churches the mere idea of imagery was suspect and they stripped their meeting halls to a stark simplicity with perhaps only an empty cross to indicate that this was a place of worship.

This was the heritage that made Jonathan Edwards wordy and dryly presented sermon popular with the masses. This is the heritage that allowed for what is now called The Age of Reason—where for good or bad, literature was the primary medium for ideas. And this is the heritage that created a Christian vacuum in art, film, and theater—and in those places where imagery reigns, a vacuum continues to exist to this day.

Not too long ago pastors, for whom *communication* of the gospel and Christian ideas were an indispensable part of their job, awoke to the fact that their flock and those who might someday respond to the message of the good news were not reacting all that positively to the time-honored way of communicating. A new language was being spoken and an old one was being lost.

Teachers in classrooms found that they had to engage kids in an active participatory manner and that the quickest way to create rebellion or to drive students away was to revert to a lecture method.

Preachers found that their listeners became listless as they waxed eloquent or plodded into deep theology but responded positively to stories, practical application, examples, object lessons, video clips, brevity, and most of all, a sense of humble honesty and authenticity.

For many who feel they don't know where to start with learning this new language or who lament the loss of the printed word as the prime medium for the exchange of ideas or motivation of the mind, the prospects are a bit terrifying. A lot of us church folks need to wrestle through some issues.

Will we be willing to suffer the loss of those people who feel that moving toward imagery and story is "dumbing down" the gospel or merely offering milk bottles to the congregation? (One ponders what ancient critics must have said about the stories of Jesus lacking depth or profundity.)

Since it is usually not in the power of one person to create the images needed to speak the new language, are we willing to change the way messages are crafted and incorporate other skilled communicators of various mediums to join the pastor in the process?

Will designing our teaching and communication using a storyboard (like animators and most filmmakers do) be something we ultimately inaugurate as a terrific way to help people get the picture?

When we discuss the crafting of a gathering, such as a Sunday morning service, the focus is not strictly on the message. In fact, our team thinks that for some people the message may not be the vehicle God uses to teach or encourage them on that morning. Images appropriate to the song being sung are imbedded to arise on the screen during a musical interlude. Brief taped and edited testimonies of the rank and file called Encounters with Christ are sometimes shown to give credence to the fact that God is active in the present as well as the past.

A montage is created with various parts and layers so that something like Communion is celebrated with action (taking the bread and cup), audio (theme appropriate worship music), images (various scenes of the Passion in both art and video), environment (the lowering of lights for a sense of soberness), and Word (passages of Scripture projected overhead). The result is an experience in which all senses come into play. Which part of the experience contributes most to the power of the moment is difficult to gauge.

Whatever we may prefer, the new language is upon us. Those churches that learn its dialect will be the ones that speak effectively to future generations. Those who don't will increasingly find themselves speaking to empty seats . . . or simply to each other.

CHAPTER 16

Contemporary Fusion

Resurrecting Tradition in the Modern Church

In 2004 Touchstone Pictures dumped over $100 million into an epic retelling of the battle of the Alamo.

It bombed at the box office.

In the postmortem agonies that studios must go through to try to figure out why a picture about an American icon that included decent actors, patriotic elements, and great action sequences would go into the tank, one of their conclusions was telling.

The studio *presumed* that people had a basic understanding of the historical background in which the fight at the Alamo had taken place, which would excite them about seeing this new version of those events. Except for perhaps Texas, they found that the average person had no idea what the battle of the Alamo was all about—and little interest in it.

We as Americans had, for all practical purposes, lost this part of our past.

As I shouldered more and more of the responsibility for the spiritual direction of the adults in our little church I came to realize that the vast majority of them were completely out of touch with any heritage of the faith they held so dearly. This lack of perspective tinted much of their thinking and led many of them to wander unthinkingly down the path of whatever was currently trendy in the Christian marketplace.

It might sound ironic coming from someone who has cast overboard most of the old models of the way church is done and lived out, but I think that in our rush to be a genuine community of faith and to speak in a contemporary tongue we must also take intentional steps to resurrect and preserve our past.

Of course not all things in the past are worth trying to rescue. Sorting through the treasures and trash and then figuring out how to best display any discovery in a compelling and interesting way in the twenty-first century is more difficult than it may seem on the surface.

Some decide that partial or half measures don't cut it, which is one motive that leads some evangelicals who seek to be in touch with their history and heritage to leave their "modern" churches and link themselves with churches steeped in ancient ritual and tradition such as those found in the Orthodox or Catholic communities. But this path is attractive only to a few. For most evangelicals the future of the church does not lie in returning whole hog to the past.

The ability to rummage through the rich attic of the Christian faith for things of value that will speak to this century takes skill and energy. It also takes a lot of time to sift through the tailings and wordiness of ancient writings in order to discover the nuggets worthy of passing on to modern saints. And it takes a person who can translate into the current experience the concepts found in some of these profound words and traditions and who can skillfully guide others to appreciate the history and heritage behind them.

Figuring out how to weld what you find seamlessly into current culture is another challenge. There is no textbook on how to salvage newly discovered bits of historic spiritual beauty nor are there vast resources readily available that have done most of the work for us. As a result, if you compare how different leaders have attempted to reach this goal, what plays out at the congregational level can be significantly and uniquely different.

Seeking a fusion of new and ancient in his church, my friend Dan Kimball, pastor at Vintage Faith Church in Santa Cruz, California, monkeyed with candles, incense, icons, and crosses to create a worship service designed to tap the senses and emotions as well as the mind.

Our crew, on the other hand, passed on the smells, bells, and candles and took a more technological track by deciding to weave into many worship gatherings bite-size meditative yet visual moments of film and music that would expose our folks to words, thoughts, deeds, and prayers of selected ancient thinkers of the church. We also created various forms of benedictions, video calls to worship, and creatively unique exposures to timeless creeds and articles of faith that are occasionally sprinkled into the worship experience.

Our expectations for this small discovery of our valuable past are modest. We hope to whet the appetite of some of our more adventurous or intellectually astute people by exposing them via modern media to meaty but small portions of Chesterton, the lofty words of Augustine, the bold declaration of a creed, or the lyrical beauty of an old prayer. If one out of ten decides to pick up *The Imitation of Christ* or *Cloud of the Unknowing* because we slid a tasty bit past their noses on Sunday morning, that's good enough for us. If tiny slivers of Pascal pop up here and there prompting a few to run out and buy *Pensées*, a tiny miracle will have taken place.

We even decided to resurrect the idea of Communion each Sunday, which, for most evangelical churches, is celebrated at various intervals or on some special occasions rather than weekly. But our solution to bringing this old practice (as old as the church herself) back as a weekly opportunity was a bit unique.

In a dimly lit room a ring of sofas surrounds the table on which the elements are set. Lyric-less guitar worship music gently fills the space. It is quiet, serene, and prayerful. Communion is self-administered and the room is open for reflection, meditation, and communion for a half hour before our large gathering launches.

Many do not take advantage of this opportunity, and we do, from time to time, have the whole family celebrate the Lord's Supper during a regular worship service. But for those inclined, the voluntary experience is powerful, meaningful, and, for some, the highlight of the morning.

We also regularly scour old hymnals for songs that can be adapted by our musicians and appreciated with a modern beat or electric instrument. We comb through the works of the early church fathers for bits of wisdom and insight that can bless people separated by thousands of years. We raid the masters of art for the images that have moved people for ages so we can drench our congregation with them via an electronic medium. We start "literary" Bible studies that have taken groups of people through Bunyan's *Pilgrim's Progress*, Augustine's *Confessions*, and Lewis's *The Great Divorce*. We use our quarterly newsletters to slide in information that, along with the goings on of the church, gives a little history lesson on things like where the English Bible came from or what the Puritans believed.

The irony is that because so many of our faithful know so little of their heritage the kernels of the past that are woven in with things of modern coinage are not often recognized as ancient. Some folks are surprised to find that the cool little closing statement projected at the end of the service was from *The Cloud of the Unknowing* penned centuries before by a Catholic mystic (who called himself Dionysius the Areopagite) instead of Max Lucado.

CHAPTER 17

A Blessing in Disguise

Creativity Unleashed

In 1992 a class 5 hurricane called Iniki swept over the entire island where I live. A class 5 hurricane means sustained winds over 150 mph. It also means naked trees, broken windows, downed power poles, flying roofs, 150 mph shingle Frisbees, fences soaring through the air along with pets, lawn furniture, and anything else not hidden in some safe pocket.

In the aftermath of the storm, entire houses lay crushed in the middle of the street. The litter of thousands of private homes, now roofless or wall-less, spread everywhere one could see, like king-size confetti. There was no water, no flushing toilets, no power, no phones, no laundry, no anything—and there would not be—for *months*.

On top of that, all 55,000 residents were absolutely stuck. There was nowhere you could drive to escape the devastation or find respite. All planes off the island were priority jammed with panicking tourists who abandoned their rent-a-cars willy-nilly and flooded the airport desperately trying to get away from the Garden Island that suddenly had become the Garbage Island.

So, like all the rest of the local residents, our family hunkered down into a quasi-Third World kind of existence. No water, no power, and lots of people suddenly homeless or squatting in blue tarp-covered shelters. We bathed daily in streams, peed in the bushes, barbecued with the neighbors for a week straight (imagine how much food there suddenly was to eat when all those freezers started defrosting), wore each article of clothing until it was filthy, went without underwear, and moved around in candlelight.

Toilets would be made functional by loading our trash cans into a truck, filling them at a nearby stream, and then doing a bucket brigade action to fill the tank of each toilet in the house. The standing rule: you flush, you fill the tank.

Other than clean up and forage, there was not much for anyone to do, no place to go, nothing to purchase, and nothing to entertain us. So we entertained ourselves. We made music, told stories, played games, and rediscovered each other. Dusty Monopoly games came off the shelves and fortunes were won or lost daily. Every member of the household became a wizard at the card game Hearts, and we invented new games such as "pain Checkers," where to lose a game piece meant to submit yourself for a pink belly. Long forgotten literary friends reappeared as in candlelight we read classic books out loud and sometimes even spooked ourselves with the tales of Edgar Allan Poe.

When the sun went down, pretty much the whole island went to bed. Life seemed to move in slow motion and people had lots of time to spend with each other. (It's my understanding that there was a bump in the birth rate nine months or so later as well.) And believe it or not, this went on for months.

In spite of the massive damage (and fortunately only one fatality), I have come to think that this hurricane was one of the best things that ever happened to our church families, and certainly my own. It taught many, many lessons and knit together all who endured that day and the aftermath.

Whole gangs of men got together and helped repair the homes of others and then rewarded themselves with a huge lunch of "Meals Ready to Eat" (the modern tasteless version of Army C-rations), provided to our church by the caseload to distribute to needy people. Families made room for folks who had lost their dwellings, and personal "stuff" became communal property.

One of the best things that happened was that the destructive might of those wind fists smashing down every power pole on the island weaned everyone cold turkey from the habit of TV viewing.

The TV is often like a tyrannical visitor whom we bring into our home for small bits of entertainment and pleasure but who ends up dominating our time and spawning offspring into every room of the house. So subtle, so addicting is TV viewing that many people wake, eat, cook, clean, try to have conversation, make love, and go to sleep with the television sound and light as constant companion—and don't think it odd.

More than that, the proliferation of images and experiences shared vicariously by the blue TV light has created a society that processes information differently; has shorter attention spans; has adopted ideas and agendas cleverly delivered, dumbed down to have the vocabulary of a twelve-year-old; and has the tendency to confuse mere personalities with men and women of substance. The tube has created a culture with a fickle appetite for knowledge or truth and one that has surrendered much personal imagination and creativity to the passivity of watching things happen rather than making them happen. Like an electronic drug, it has allowed people to be entertained with no effort rather than stimulating people to discover how to entertain and interest themselves.

But go without the tube for three months—and without power to drive any other systems of entertainment—and the resultant weaning is revolutionary. One discovers that conversation is more fun and stimulating than corporate staring. One realizes that without TV you have no idea which personality is currently cool, what show is the must-see, and you find that it doesn't matter a whit in real life. Doing becomes far more fun than watching, creating more interesting than observing, activity more vibrant than passivity.

If, as the statistics say, most people spend eight years of their life watching TV, going without it made many of us realize what a pathetic squandering of time and opportunity that is. After the power came back on, many of us chose to stay weaned.

And what a difference it has made. Without the marketing connected to cartoon programs, my children have no idea what toy to ask for at Christmastime. Without the easy distraction of TV, many books have been read, projects embarked on, and conversations held.

I find it interesting that all four of our kids play music, are deeply involved in crafts and hobbies, and are voracious readers. Our eldest, after immersion in the *Lord of the Rings* trilogy (the books, not the movies) taught himself to read, write, and speak Elvish—which comes in handy if you meet some elves. How much of this would have erupted had the cable hookup been active, I don't know, but I suspect far less.

Most fascinating of all, I do not hear those two words that seem to be standard with those who depend on others for their amusement: "I'm bored!"

I bring up the illustration of television not to bash the banal content or its ability to play to the lazy path of least resistance in our choice of recreation and entertainment. These things are self-evident. But I chose this example because it is merely *one* obvious and ubiquitous area where our culture has surrendered its imagination and creativity for the prepackaged, easy access, just-add-water kind of fare that is attractively placed right at our fingertips.

The disturbing thing is that the Christian church, along with the rest of the secular culture, long ago surrendered her imagination. And the result has been a kind of faith that is often dull, uninspired, clone prone, and dependent upon a few creative minds to do all the heavy lifting.

Personally, I have this sneaking suspicion that the God we serve is wildly imaginative and creative. I also suspect that the process of becoming transformed into His image is not only one of increasing in personal holiness but of taking on other family traits as well, such as a God-breathed imagination.

This process, so aptly described to the folks in Corinth by the apostle Paul in these words: "And so we are transfigured much like the Messiah, our lives gradually becoming brighter and more beautiful as God enters our lives and we become like him" (2 Corinthians 3:18, MSG), is one which ought to serve the church by making her full of not only the most caring bunch of characters in town but the most outrageously creative and inspired gang of people as well!

But imagination and creativity are not talked about much in church circles. They are not particularly sought-after virtues. Instead, we become consumers of the bright ideas of the few people knighted to be our creative thinkers.

But what would happen if churches got into the business of celebrating creativity?

What would happen if we became the publisher for the writers in our midst or used our walls to display the work of our artists or hired our high school computer hotshots to create and run our websites?

What if we took all of our most creative types and threw them in a room with food, drink, a budget, and an objective such as how to reach new people with the gospel or make the worship service more engaging? And what if they knew we would actually *attempt* to do the things that they suggested? What might we beget with that kind of unleashed creativity?

What if we banished all curricula for a month and made our teachers invent their own lessons based on a selection of Scripture? Would our kids be hurt or helped? Would our teachers have more or less ownership?

What if we could convince our people that unplugging the

TV in their home might be a *good* thing for their family, their love life, their souls, and their intellect? What if we went so far as to pass out pledge cards so that people would commit to go without watching TV programs for various amounts of time in the next year (one month intervals up to a year without the tube)?

Would tinkering around with all these things make us a stronger, more imaginative people in the end?

Among the people we work with, the imagination bar is high. The musicians better not come to us wanting to record a praise worship CD of cover songs. If you can't be creative enough to write your own music we aren't going to spend church funds on the project.

Our growing "unplugged club" has a book exchange going and makes jokes with those who can't quite take the big step to disconnect, calling them "American Idle."

Interestingly, some of the projects created for internal use by our artists, musicians, and writers have escaped the island and found a wider audience, being picked up by established publishing or music companies.

During those three months without power I received a blessing in disguise. I was reminded of the difference between being entertained and entertaining one's self. I was reminded of the difference between being a tourist and a traveler, between being a consumer and a creator, a person who watches things happen and a person who makes things happen. It was a valuable lesson on a personal level. I have a hunch, no, a conviction, that it might be a valuable lesson to the church as well.

CHAPTER 18

A Family Meal

Serving the Tastiest Fare

Even in these times of fast food and demanding schedules most people still find it possible to sit down now and then for a family meal. What if we were to use the family meal as a template to rethink our worship gatherings?

What do we want our gathering times to be? Who do we want to be there? What do we honestly suppose they will take from the table?

As a kid I was often forced to go to "big church." It was serious, solemn, and full of unfathomable ritual, long boring lectures and unsingable music. They also had pew cards and small dull-pointed pencils a young kid could use as entertainment. I probably owe my cartooning abilities in part to boring hours spent drawing on the backs of countless pew cards.

The logic of the day dictated that while you might be bored out of your mind at church, someday you would wake up to appreciate and enjoy it all. Kind of like broccoli. As I grew up the opposite happened; the taste never developed and as soon as I could, I left church behind.

My response probably would have been very different if the family meal template had been used. Some families lay the spread out on the table and pass around the bowls of food, some use a cafeteria style and lay out the food on the counter so the family can pass by on a self-serve mission, and some sit around a table and spin the lazy Susan. In some families the patriarch is the *only* one who is allowed to carve the roast; in others it is a free-for-all.

For some, the family meal means a call for the best dishes while in other households a family meal means a barbecue while enjoying the informality of paper plates and plastic cups.

In most homes, a visitor who happens to be present for a family meal is simply grafted in for the moment and made to feel as if they belong—except for the fact that they are usually allotted a place first in line.

Growing up, our family mealtimes always included a nice fresh tablecloth, several candles dripping wax (for the kids to play with), and a dog under the table who was happy to gulp down any portion deemed undesirable or too vast to completely consume.

Preparing for the family meal usually involved everyone. Mom would be creating her magic over the stove; Dad would be busy making up his special brand of "make you sweat salsa" or fiddling with the coffee brewer. Siblings would be drafted to set the table. After the meal, it was understood that the gang would jump in again to clear and clean up.

One interesting but often overlooked thing about family meals is the food choice. Among the mounds and mounds of food served, very rarely is there to be found something that would be considered a gourmet specialty. No snails, unpronounceable fruit, strange pungent oddities. Most of the time, Mom, in her infinite wisdom, realized that family meals are for *families*, and if you want the family to enjoy the food and time together then the dishes prepared and served should be those that everyone would be most likely to enjoy.

Now that doesn't mean that Junior won't turn up his nose at the broccoli or that Uncle Eddie won't pick all the tomatoes out of his salad, but by and large what is cooked up, while tasty and nourishing, is designed for *family* palates—kids through adults, and not for those with a taste for the refined or obscure.

For those whose sense of adventure leads them to nibbling on Yak cheese or munching on octopus tentacles, well, there are other places to do that besides the family meal. And any Mom who rolls out the bizarre delicacies at a family meal is inviting howls of protest, aghast faces, and empty stomachs.

Now if you have a church full of spiritual connoisseurs, then serving up rarified delicacies from the Word is not likely to be a problem. But most churches have far more in common with a family meal. We have young and old, we have family and visitors, we have spiritual babes and spiritual veterans, we have those who want to be there and those who would rather be somewhere else, we have those with big spiritual appetites and those with barely any hunger at all. We have those who don't need to learn new theological truths so much as they need to be buoyed up with simple hope. We have those whose lives are a train wreck and those whose lives are happy land. We have the witty and the dull, the wise and the foolish, the shining stars and the oddballs.

Just like a big extended family.

So what do we serve up? Finely chopped theology niceties? A hearty dose of God-sprinkled guilt? Indigestible dredgings from deep Bible? Verse-by-verse musings with hardly a "so what" attached? Stuff that our people have to pick through to find anything palatable to remember, apply, or take home, often overcooked (or undercooked) in the oven of delivery for way too long?

It is my firm belief that if we consider our worship gatherings to be something we want (for the most part) all the family to be at, then we are obligated to provide the kind of healthy spiritual nourishment that the majority can consume without difficulty.

For example, if we want high school students to be at the Sunday family meal, then we need to make sure that they won't just pick at what is presented. If we want all varieties of spiritual maturity to be fed, then we won't deliver or package our worship service to be difficult or inaccessible to the uninitiated. If we want to make sure that we present something that will be lasting nourishment to the soul, we need to work hard at creating messages and moments that have high retention value and answer the big "SO WHATS?" that ought to come out of being challenged by God's Word.

Start thinking this way and things are gonna change. The connoisseurs will run off to the First Church of Spiritual Delectables down the road. The "we've always done it this way" crowd will squawk and peck. Some of our weird uncles will show their weirdness. But finally, the regular common folk are going to have a tasty family meal that both nourishes and sticks to their ribs!

What might this stick-to-the-ribs spiritual meal look like?

For us it means keeping it simple to comprehend or digest. A simple idea is not the same as a stupid one. Simple concepts can be terrifyingly difficult in their ramifications.

This meal has to be compelling as well. I am told that Limburger cheese tastes quite good once you get it past your nose. I will never know—I simply can't get that smell of toe jam past my olfactory lobe.

A good family meal at church is one that seems right off the bat to be something of interest, something inviting, like the layer of melted cheese that covers a casserole. Sometimes a story and illustration, a visual image or a prop is the very thing needed to arouse hunger toward what is being served up. But deviating on to some long bunny trail or launching a screeching rendition of "His Eye is on the Sparrow" makes it tough to get people back to the table mentally.

We, and probably most people who attend church, think short is good. Better to leave people wishing for more than overstuffed.

One point is good too. I am not sure who invented three-point sermons but few can remember them twenty minutes after a worship gathering. Better one point from three different vantage points.

Practical is also good—everyday life practical.

I like to imagine that the meal served up each Sunday is like what spinach is to Popeye. Wham! It goes right where it is needed most, when it is needed most!

CHAPTER 19

All Together Now

Carol Power

It started off as a wild-hair dinner idea.

I was scratching hard to come up with a novel, effective, and fun way to help new folks in our church get to know each other and some key regulars by sharing some flaming barbecue ribs and a "touch" of something personal—but not scary personal.

I sat in front of the blank computer screen, hopefully rubbing an empty Dr. Pepper can like Aladdin's lamp when the idea popped. My fingers flew to the keys!

The invitation to the party, as well as date, time, and location included the following instructions: *"And for something completely different, please imagine that you have been banished to a desert island for an indefinite future. You have been given a solar-driven CD player but you are only allowed to bring ONE CD with you. Which would it be? Please grab that CD and bring it along with you (we may want to play it) . . . and if it is the Grateful Dead's Greatest Hits or anything by*

Michael Jackson, be prepared to explain yourself. Heck, be prepared to explain anyhow!"

Now being a self-proclaimed clever guy, I thought that this would be a sneaky and entertaining way to get to know something about these new folks without anyone having to do serious gut spilling; a safe and fun glimpse into new lives, a quick and painless peek into the front door of each person but no serious rummaging through the dresser drawers of their souls.

Boy, was I wrong.

I was shocked and unprepared for what happened at that party. Somehow through this silly device I had unwittingly tapped into a jugular vein of human emotion.

In retrospect, I realized I should have anticipated it. After all, music can be far more than mere entertainment. It can be the milestone or rallying point for the most important events in our lives. The special song that recalls our childhood or high school days, the tune that makes us think about a valued person in our lives, those little slivers of music that are firmly tied to memories both good and bad.

But here is the shocker: over half of the people who attended the barbecue brought *Christmas* CDs—carols, old, old songs. (I, on the other hand, mysteriously brought *Leif and Liege* by Fairport Convention.)

Each person, in turn, went to the CD player and played a cut or two from the album they had brought. Then they started to share why they picked that particular CD. Those who had chosen CDs of Christmas carols to accompany them on their banishment described their selection in a beautiful way that made perfectly good sense.

These were songs of faith. Remember the words of most of the old favorite yuletide tunes? They all celebrate God's love, the incarnation, the mission, and majesty. Just recall the last stanza of "Hark the Herald Angels Sing."

> Hail, the heaven-born Prince of peace!
> Hail the Sun of righteousness!
> Light and life to all he brings,
> risen with healing in his wings.
> Mild he lays his glory by,
> born that man no more may die,
> born to raise the sons of earth,
> born to give them second birth.
> Hark! the herald angels sing,
> Glory to the newborn King.

Now there, hiding in a common Christmas carol, is a powerful piece of theology!

These were songs of remembrance. These were songs that triggered vivid and cherished memories of family, joy, and childhood innocence, golden tinted moments of time that Christmas carols help to resurrect. The faces of people no longer in this world present themselves in the height of kindred celebration and warmth via these tunes.

These were songs of solidarity. These were songs that, in a culture so musically divided, we all come together on: the rappers, country-western singers, classical music buffs, and punk rockers. All the important things about God, faith, and family intersected in these well-worn Christmas carols.

As people began to explain why they brought their Christmas CDs there was the distinct choking of emotion in many voices. Deeply personal statements slipped out.

"My father always loved to sing 'Deck the Halls' at Christmastime," one woman said. "He would be putting up the tree or hanging the lights singing that silly song at the top of his lungs. Even though he is gone, I always think of him at Christmas."

Deep, powerful stuff.

The result of this meal (besides sticky fingers) was a decision that the next CD our church produced would not be a collection of cool praise and worship songs but rather a Christmas CD full of the old classics. And that we would print enough to make sure that every family in our community got one free.

Because we know they will be listening, remembering, and opening the crack in the door to that Someone much bigger than themselves—if not during exile on a desert island, at least every year right around Christmastime.

CHAPTER 20

Light Bearers, Grace Mongers, and Peddlers of Hope

Our Divine Nuisance Crew

As a pastor, I like people to go to church. In particular, I prefer that they go to *our* church rather than the church up the street. The more people who show up on a Sunday morning the more successful I feel at doing my job.

And regardless of what any pastor *tells* you about numbers not being important or the spiel they might hand out about valuing quality over quantity, they are kidding themselves if, in their heart of hearts, they don't secretly wish for their church to be increasing in attendees.

Most of us will take any new folks we can get, even at the expense of some other church that is imploding or going through a hard patch. But most of us would much rather grow with people who are either new to the community or, best of all, new to the faith! Attracting the latter takes the most energy, challenge, and creative thought of all and is therefore typically the least practiced way of growth. Effective evangelism is a moving target. It mutates from time to time, making today's successful methods tomorrow's flops.

We usually think in terms of getting people to *come to us*. "If I can only get so and so to come to church," we reason, "then he will find the Lord."

But so and so probably won't be coming to church.

Our leadership team has taken great and imaginative measures to ensure that the entry ramp into the life of Christian community is easy to navigate and welcoming for those taking their first and usually very hesitant steps into the scary world of "church people." If I do say so myself, Kauai Christian Fellowship is a warm, upbeat, user friendly, nonthreatening, food-and-coffee-laden atmosphere that the average person would have to try very hard to dislike.

Even so, from the vast sea of the unchurched we are getting only a drop in the bucket to *come to us*. The more I think about it, the more I am convinced that while it is a great thing to get those who are unsaved into church, it is equally important for the church to get out into the realm of the unsaved by doing something effective, meaningful, and personal. Or, in other words, rather than just inflate the church with people coming from the world, it is equally important to inflate the world with people coming from the church. We must make an impact for the gospel among people for whom coming to church would be the last stop on their list.

Suppose for a moment that Christians saw it as their *mission* in life not merely to be good churchgoing people but *light bearers*, *grace mongers*, and *peddlers of hope* to a dark, screwy world. What if it were an *intentional strategy* for the church to step into the everyday world with blessings and grace? What if the motto of St. Francis, "Preach the gospel at all times and if necessary, use words," was our loudest "battle cry"? What if we began to make the love of Jesus known in small, simple, personal, and elegant ways?

My guess is that God would start to work in many of the lives we touch. The good infection would catch and spread. Even for those who want to resist the gospel of Jesus, there would be at every turn an inescapable divine nuisance.

What might this look like?

We have a little group who are self-designated agitators of love, sowers of the seeds of grace, and wreakers of divine havoc. They spend time thinking of how we can make someone's day a little brighter—particularly someone who doesn't care much for church. They try to come up with how we, the local church community, can show appreciation to those who feel taken for granted, celebrate those who work quietly in invisible or thankless jobs, and spread joy around town in the name of Jesus.

They started by preparing a delicious lunch for every school teacher at our local elementary school simply to say, "We know that as teachers you get a lot of frustration from parents and little praise, but we notice and appreciate what you do." No tracts, no Bible verses, no invitations to the church. Just a simple act of appreciation from the community of faith they live and work near.

Now imagine for a minute being on the receiving end of that lunch. Whatever negative encounters an unbelieving teacher might have had with Christians in the past can suddenly be checkmated by a sandwich given in the same kind of love Jesus gave—the unconditional kind. Whatever the day holds for a teacher there has been one bright spot—an actual free lunch!

What do you suppose is most effective in influencing people to become open to things of God? You might ask the folks who work at our local Taco Bell what a little loving and caring can do. Virtually all the workers are foreign born, their English is halting, and they are working hard in the back for minimum wage. They are the invisible men and women for most of us. The least likely to darken the doors of *our* church or show up at *our* events. The least likely to live in *our* neighborhoods or attend *our* schools.

So they were the perfect target for our Divine Nuisance Crew.

Finding out how many employees our Taco Bell had from a casual conversation with the manager, the gang showed up one midafternoon, after the lunch rush, with a gift bag for every worker. In each bag were edible treats, a gift certificate to the local theater, various goodies, and a handwritten card to say thank you for all the hard work from a group of people who actually do notice.

No strings. No Christian books or CDs. No gimmicks. Just a paper-bag token that says that those who are working behind the counter at Taco Bell are noticed.

Does it "work"?

How can one measure?

Do the taco folks show up at church? Sometimes—and sometimes not for a long time. But if the Taco Bell workers go home and treat their spouse or kids better because someone, in the name of Jesus, loved and noticed them today, that is good enough for our Divine Nuisance Crew. If they awaken a bit more to God's all-giving love and become a little better human being, that's good enough. If they are pleased and yet puzzled, that's good enough. If the givers are more blessed than the receivers, that's good enough.

Just imagine how annoying it would be for someone who is trying to resist or ignore God to keep having believers pop up in places where believers are normally mute and do good things in the name of their Lord! Imagine what could happen if, unfettered from the church building, followers of Jesus started to get involved in sharing a message of caring with their neighbors.

The church should pop up in action here and there in our secular world all the time. Our caring influence, authentic compassion, and kind consideration will earn us the right to be heard far quicker than any fire-breathing attack on the foibles of unbelief.

There are probably lots of ways to do this, both corporate and individual. But our Lord doesn't really give us the option to merely enjoy each other's company in the privacy of our fellowship group. That's no doubt why He gave these marching instructions: "Let your light shine before men, that they may see your good deeds and praise your Father in heaven" (Matthew 5:16).

CHAPTER 21

Drawing on the Walls

Becoming a Permission-Giving Church

I never aspired to be a pastor, nor did I ever imagine that I would end up doing any writing. But from the time I can remember, I always figured I was going to be a cartoonist.

My love affair with cartoons started with old black-and-white Popeye cartoons shown during those precious two hours of the day that the ancient networks devoted to kids. It progressed with the Sunday comics, comic books by the ton, and *MAD Magazine*.

As a kid I drew cartoons all the time, I talked my high school art teacher into letting me forgo the curriculum at hand to spend my time in class doing nothing but cartooning, and as I go back and look at the remnants of college class notes I can see where the professor failed to keep my attention; the page morphs from block printed notes into cartoons of all shapes and sizes. I still enjoy drawing cartoons and often use them in various ways both as teaching tools and for publication.

My journey toward considering myself a serious candidate as a cartoonist can be traced back to a single incident that took place when I was around five or six years old.

The lady next door was a widow. In her eighties, she patiently and lovingly put up with the antics of all the mischievous little rascals popping out of the baby-making ovens of the fifties—the offspring now called the Baby Boomers. None of us knew the old lady by her given name. All the kids affectionately called her Mom Hyatt.

Now, every child is an artist, it's just that in growing up we sometimes forget what we once were. Our little art neighborhood colony would often get bored with staying in the lines of the coloring book and grab some chalk and create murals on the sidewalk or design a dandy mud sculpture. Whenever we would make a creation the next act was to trudge over to Mom Hyatt's humble little cottage to proudly show off our latest masterpiece to the "oohs" and "ahhs" of her praise.

One summer morning while showing off some doodle to Mom Hyatt, I noticed that one wall of her living room seemed barren and void of obstacles such as doors or cupboards. In childish innocence I asked if she would allow me to draw pictures on her wall. The old lady thought for a moment and then kindly replied, "Why, yes, I would be very pleased to have you create a mural on my wall."

For the next few days I returned to the wall with my crayons. It would be an underwater scene complete with cartoon-looking fish, eels, an octopus, seaweed, and sharks. I labored diligently, spreading the colored wax on the elderly woman's living room wall.

I never told anyone what I was doing. My mother knew I was going next door to draw pictures but even at that age I was aware that it was a magic moment and the opportunity to actually draw on someone's living room wall might be lost if I opened my mouth.

When the project was done, Mom Hyatt put her hand on my small shoulder and with great enthusiasm proclaimed, "This is the best mural I have ever seen! Why, Rick, I can tell you are going to be a wonderful cartoonist."

The work was raw, amateurish, and silly. I really wasn't much of a cartoonist—I just thought I was.

Everyone in the neighborhood was brought in to admire the sea mural on Mom Hyatt's living room wall. My mother said it was very nice and then lovingly tried to reprove the old lady for being such a softy.

"I don't have that much time left," said Mom Hyatt, "and the drawings of children bring me a lot of happiness."

My mom couldn't argue with that one. And I proudly strutted back home believing that I was destined to be a cartoonist.

The destiny came to be realized. The fact is I am a cartoonist with my work published in national magazines and books as well as showing up on a lot of the things I do in church. (Guess who designs many of our camp T-shirts?) Although I never had the raw, inborn talent that some of my illustrator heroes had, I had something else that kept me going: the trust, encouragement, and faith of someone who said "yes" to a request that most women would have turned down.

I think Mom Hyatt was on to something. (My mural stayed on her wall until the day of her death.) That old woman knew something that would be good for churches to remember: We nurture the future by being a place that dares to say yes when others would say no.

Churches are not often seen as permission-giving places. They are not places where you imagine that you will quickly get a "yes" to a request. Our decision-making groups often are seen by people as a collection of folks who are naturally inclined to say "no" and must be convinced in order to get buy-in on an idea. And when people think the answer will likely be "no," they're much less likely to bother asking. As a result, not a whole lot of things take place that are spontaneous or quickly planned.

We have a few acres of undeveloped land. No doubt we will be using it in the future but for now it makes a nice place for weeds to grow. So when the young man showed up at our leadership meeting early one Tuesday and said he had a bright idea to make a BMX track in the weed patch it took about a minute and a half for him to get the green light. Just covering a few safety issues and how the track would be used in ministry were the key concerns. The next thing you know a little Bobcat was building mounds of dirt and scraping away the track for all the smiley kids with dusty faces.

And when the young mother came and asked if she could paint a mural on all the walls of the brand new nursery, well, how do you say "no" to that when your own art career started in a similar way?

"Had she ever done a mural before?" we asked. "No" this would be her first one. "Okay," we responded, "but how about doing it one wall at a time?"

The young woman left beaming.

"What if she can't pull it off?" some practical thinker in the group asked.

"Well, it's better to pay for a gallon of paint to repaint the wall than to discourage someone who has a vision," was the consensus.

The mural is done, and it ain't bad for a first big art project. And the tykes in the nursery have yet to complain.

It takes a specific mindset and intention to create an environment that is eager to say "yes!" to new ideas and ministries. It means taking away veto power from those who are skittish about novelty and change. It means streamlining the way from point A to point B. It means having a quick "yes/go" type of decision-making process put in place. It means that not everyone gets to weigh in before something is launched. It means we need to trust the folks who allowed and authorized the thing without our getting to sign off on it. It means being willing to take a gamble from time to time and being willing to pay the price necessary if the gamble doesn't work out. It means being flame fanners instead of wet blankets.

Dare to become this kind of church and see what happens. People with ideas will find you out. Doers will find their way to you because at least they will have a chance to *do* something without having to wade through mountains of red tape. You will get a reputation as a place that encourages things to happen, that wants to believe in your people, and that is willing to let folks draw on your walls.

CHAPTER 22

Never Scrapped

What the Success Stories Don't Tell You

History is always written by victors.

Imagine the way things would be taught about our involvement in World War II if somehow the Nazis came out on top, or the new spin on things that would come if the American Indians had run the immigrants back into the sea.

Church and Christian life success books are usually written by the victors as well. They are written by (or ghostwritten for) the pastor of the megachurch; the successful sounding traveling speaker; or the high-profile couple with perfect children; perfect marriage; and perfect hair. And the things most of these books don't tell you about are the failures and foot shootings incurred while en route to the best marriage, best church, best ministry, or best family in the world.

That's because failing doesn't sell.

We celebrate those who made it to the top of Everest in 1953 and find the name of Hillary emblazoned on outdoor products for years to come, but we have no interest in those whose expeditions up the same peak ended in failure (or for that matter Tenzing Norgay, the Sherpa who was with Hillary all the way and without whom the ascent would have been doomed). They are nobodies in the cosmic world of marketing compared with Sir Edmund.

Thomas Edison is said to have failed 1,200 times before successfully coming up with the lightbulb. So cork-like was Edison's optimism that he is quoted as saying, "I have not failed. I've just found 10,000 ways that won't work." But Edison is celebrated, in the end, not because of his failures but because one of his experiments *did* finally work!

But most people can't survive thousands of failed attempts. Even a few failings are enough to take the wind out of most of our sails. What many people who write these victorious books don't mention is that risk and failure often sleep in the same bed.

Lest anyone reading this book gets the idea that every wild idea I have come up with has been a winner or that I belong to some anointed club that has the Midas touch of ministry, let me be quick to point out that I have conducted Bible studies where I was the only attendee, planned youth activities that crashed straight into the ground, hosted concerts that cost the church its financial shorts, and given messages that weren't worth getting up for. I've tried and failed to reach some people and ignored others who were eager to be reached. I've had more than my share of mixed results, so-so consequences, and bangs not even closely equal to the buck they cost.

Risk and failure not only sleep in the same bed but sometimes failure takes all the covers.

While failing at times to measure up anywhere close to excellence in ministry is always a low blow to the ego, even worse is acknowledging a failure of character. That admission feels like a stake in the heart. But I have a hunch that being well versed in personal failures may be as essential for leading and ministering to others effectively as anything else we can cook up. Being a bit of a spiritual cripple keeps one from thinking of oneself as a spiritual champion.

The apostle Peter was dealt a crushing blow to his imagined strength in the hours prior to Jesus' crucifixion. But it may well be that this tough purging of self-reliance is exactly what Peter needed to be the leader of the fledgling church.

Now I know that this is not the model for a leader that we have come to desire in our local churches. We want a shining example of uncompromised strength, unlimited determination, and unwavering faith. The problem is, I don't know anybody like that. And, to be honest, the ones who are projecting that image are scary to me simply because I suspect they are either posers or naive—or both.

As for me, well, the go-for-broke Lone Ranger gallop that in the past served to insulate me from both those seeking my heart and those offering accountability had to screech to a halt. Trampling pedestrians as collateral damage in order to get to some goal exposed my skewed value system. Ultimately it wasn't good enough just to talk about being a "team player." I could talk the talk and win others to *my* team, but I've had to learn, sometimes painfully, to become a team player myself.

Failed leaders are not necessarily a problem. Leaders who think they are above failure definitely are.

Perhaps because my island home is far removed from the gossipy communication lines on the mainland or perhaps because the promise of healing in the visual beauty of Hawaii is so compelling, our little church has become home to a number of failed church leaders. Some of the failures have been severe, worthy of punishment by jail time. Some failures have been excruciatingly painful and life-altering tragedies. Some of the leaders created their own failures and some were terribly wounded and brought to failure by the explosion of a life close to their own. Some situations could have been prevented, some not.

Perhaps because our staff has experienced some classic failures among us (a few divorces, breakdowns, drug addictions, and general all around bad behavior are mixed in the heritage of our six leaders), we seem to provide a safer haven for the downfallen than most churches.

Maybe it's because of the folk who may plop down next to any one of us in our little church. Sitting in the congregation are ex-topless dancers, men who have been wife beaters, women who have been husband abusers, those with adultery or abortions on their record, those whose bodies have been given cheaply or taken violently, those who have been tormented by various addictions, those who wrestle with integrity, and a collective host of other dark issues.

Possibly it is the willingness of the people with whom one breaks bread to readily admit complete and utter failure that makes them attractive. They are tender souls who honestly think that the words "oh wretched man that I am" were written specifically with them in mind. I find it refreshing and liberating to commune with a group of people who are more than willing to vote themselves a screwup than to play the holier than thou game. Perhaps it is because we don't believe that God throws away sinful and fouled-up folks, that failed and hurting Christians seem drawn to our congregation.

Most all of us have a natural distaste for those who obviously and publicly take a moral or spiritual belly flop but try to hide their failure or brush off or belittle the enormity of their foul-up with comments like "we all make mistakes." What we really want to see is a little of the mindset Peter reflected when he yelped, "Go away from me, Lord; I am a sinful man!" (Luke 5:8), coupled with a willingness to go to the penalty box for a while, if necessary. Failing doesn't mean that we are of no use to God. In fact, it is getting to this point in recognizing our failure that marks the road back to usefulness.

As a small child, our youngest son, Hudson, was a train nut. He ate, drank, and breathed choo-choo trains. As a logical result, our home was filled with Thomas the Tank Engine toys, books, and videos.

There was something beguiling about the stories of this little train and his friends that had a familiar "Godlike" ring to them. So I did a little investigation of the author and found that he was a Christian clergyman from England named A. W. Awdry, and he had invented these little train stories to entertain his own son while the child was ill.

Explaining his treatment of the various personalities (all disguised as railroad engines) in his stories, Awdry made an interesting comment. He said, "The important thing is that the engines are punished and forgiven—but never scrapped!"

Now there is a perfect description of how the church is to deal with personal failure. Punished if need be, forgiven as called for—but never scrapped!

As the body of Christ, one of our biggest struggles is how to deal with failings and failures. Do we *really* believe that every person, no matter how horrific his or her act of failure or character was, cannot only be forgiven but also be made useful for the Kingdom? Of course we all say yes until we play the game of Monster. What one comes up with at the end of the game tells if we can do more than just repeat nice Christian platitudes.

Perhaps you would like to play Monster and see how you do. Here is the game.

You are on the leadership team at your local church. A man shows up at your church, well-worn Bible in hand but a stranger to everyone. No family or friends accompany him.

After a few visits he asks, without sharing his agenda, to make an appointment with the governing group of your church. Permission is given and at the meeting this visitor shares his story. He explains that he has recently been released from prison after a long sentence. He has no friends or family left and found your church by looking in the phone book. During his incarceration he became a Christian, came to grips with his sin, sought help for his failings, and has been following the Lord faithfully ever since. He explains that after a few visits he can see that your church is a redemptive community that wants to honor Christ, and his desire is not merely to attend a good church but to have a spiritual home, a community to belong to, and some kind of role to play or service to perform. He says that he is coming before you today to see if he would be *welcomed* into the church.

And he also thinks that you, the leaders, need to know that he was sent to prison after being convicted of sexual abuse of a minor by a person in a position of trust. With deep sorrow he recounts the horror of being a summer camp counselor who manipulated and molested a fifteen-year-old boy under his care. Because of his own untreated sexual abuse as a young teen, he had become a very sick and sinful young man and had caused irreparable harm for which he had been justly punished. Now, after many years of therapy and spiritual growth as a committed Christian, he is looking for a place in God's family where he can be both useful and nurtured.

Would this man be *welcomed* in your church?

If he was faithful and committed would he be given any responsibility or appropriate role to play in the life of your church?

Would he be treated differently?

Would he be marked as a Monster?

Would he be invited to your home, to mingle with your family? To church events that include children?

Would you rather he went to some other church?

Would you rather he be scrapped?

Yes, this child molester example is pushing the envelope to the extreme, but at Kauai Christian Fellowship we have had to wrestle through very tough issues like these with the walking and stumbling failures that come our way.

How we resolve protecting our church members is a sober duty. And even protecting our particular "monster" so he or she is not tempted to sin must be seen as an act of love instead of fear. But these critical and practical issues are not as important as the overarching mindset we choose to have toward those whose lives are marked by severe failure.

Will these folks be welcomed, cared for, and given an appropriate place to serve and grow—or will we send them to the scrap heap?

CHAPTER 23

The Treasures of the Church

Human Resources

Lawrence was a deacon of the Roman church during the days of the Emperor Valerian.

Four days earlier his pastor had been arrested and quickly executed by Roman soldiers acting on orders of the one who wore the purple. Knowing that other leaders were being rounded up, Lawrence took it upon himself to divest the church coffers of any cash by quickly distributing what little they had to the needy and destitute.

Valerian's court somehow got wind of this activity and, assuming that he would reap a windfall of riches by plundering the church, the Emperor commanded the deacon to appear before the royal court and bring with him the treasures of the church. Of course there was scant money in the early church and what was once there was now gone, but Lawrence bravely decided to appear before Valerian anyhow.

Gathering from all around Rome the members of the church who were slaves, poverty stricken, crippled, ill, and aged, he made his way up Palatine Hill. Valerian, befuddled by the great crowd of beggars following behind Deacon Lawrence, demanded that he surrender the treasures of the church.

Sweeping his arm toward the motley collection of saints piled in front of the Emperor, Lawrence declared loudly, "These are the treasures of the church."

Enraged and unimpressed by the irony of the statement, Valerian immediately sent Lawrence off to torture. Later his remains were collected by his "treasures" and buried in a cemetery off the Via Tiburtina, a place where the first Christian emperor, Constantine, would later choose to build a Basilica.

The admittedly confrontational actions of Lawrence may, upon consideration, prod our thoughts on the subject. What would we consider the treasures of our church? Our building? Our unique doctrinal positions? Our traditions (or lack of them)? Our eloquent pastor? Our history?

Sadly, the actions of the church have often reflected a misguided placement of value. We tend to treasure what is meant to be used for the Kingdom and use what is meant to be treasured.

The church building is often seen as the greatest treasure of the church. Vast amounts of money go into rooms that are occupied for an hour or two a week. We let people know that this part of the church has been set apart as a "sanctuary." But just try to let a few homeless guys find sanctuary from the cold streets by stretching out on the pews and you will find how fast that term becomes a thin parody. Mortuary might be a better term as it is dead space most of the time.

Clearly some folks treasure stuff. But stuff, even our church stuff, is not to be seen as a treasure to protect but a resource to be risked and used for Kingdom purposes. (Treasuring church stuff is often confused with "stewardship," which means using stuff with wisdom.) Jesus spelled out the principle clearly in His marvelous parable about the three servants who were entrusted with some of their master's resources and then told to use it to make investments that would further his empire (see Luke 19:11-27).

It seems to me that many times we would rather present God with a pristine building showing how thorough our protection of His assets has been rather than a well-worn, dinged up, hand-printed building showing how much service has been rendered in His name. Buildings are an easier treasure to honor than ministry. They are tangible.

Our "way of doing things" can easily become the object of our worship. We pride ourselves on our distinctions, especially our theological or methodological distinctions, and make those distinctions the treasure we worship instead of treasuring those essential things that we have in common with all believers. In fact, we often haul out our idiosyncratic treasures and compare our way of doing worship (altar call or no altar call), our theology (filled, baptized, or indwelt), our method (sprinkled, dunked, or hosed), with the obvious poverty of others.

But Jesus didn't die for our buildings. He was not sacrificed for our distinctions or our traditions. He came for the real treasure: people. "Where your treasure is," He said, "there your heart will be also" (Matthew 6:21).

I would imagine that upon reflection, most of us would come to the same conclusion. The treasure of the church can usually be located sitting right next to us in rumpled clothing or there upwind of us, reeking of too much cheap perfume on Sunday morning. The greatest treasure of the church was and continues to be the simple, often the have-nots, those who figure they have little to give but will give whatever they have unrestrainedly.

Faces come to mind when I think of those treasures. I see a chain-smoking, tattooed Colin squinting under his filthy baseball cap as he and his equally grubby pal Jimbo faithfully mow the lawn that surrounds the church campus on their time off. I see Susie, who survived breast cancer, reaching out to other women in the community who have heard their doctor say, "I'm afraid I have some bad news for you." I see Holly all by herself in the nursery on Monday mornings carefully cleaning the toddlers' toys. I see Skip, drill in hand, who came out of retirement to serve as Mr. Fixit. I see Bob and Gloria cleaning urinals, toilets, and sinks each Saturday morning. And I see the faces of countless others who, for no other reason than their love of Jesus, have offered what they have to His service.

We pastors are not the treasures of the church but rather prospectors whose job it is to unearth these precious ones and bring their worth to the light of day. Not all of the treasures lay on the surface; some take digging and prodding to be released. And as with literal treasure, a bit of buffing and polishing truly brings out the beauty and worth of the fortune God has placed in each congregation.

As I have become aware of the immense riches in the people

God has gathered, I have become a strong proponent of buffing out and celebrating these unsung heroes at every turn. I love it that the congregation claps for the worship band—a clap that is both saying "thank you" to the band and "thank you" to God at the same time.

We have made it a habit to announce weekly the hidden deeds and activities of our bashful treasures. From time to time we ambush one of our unseen workers with a full-blown, all-church appreciation party—balloons, signs, cake, cards, and all. They hate the attention, which makes their beauty shine all the brighter.

When we step into eternity we may be surprised at those who are considered treasures. I suspect that in most cases it is *not* going to be the minister of a megachurch or the brilliant theological scrapper. I doubt it will be the bright lights of Christian celebrity-hood or those who have an easy way with words, music, or voice. I think we may be celebrating the arrival into the Kingdom of a tattooed, sun-wrinkled man wearing a filthy baseball cap, cigarette dangling from his lips, riding down the streets of gold on a lawn mower—which was his unnoticed, but wholehearted, faithful and worthy offering to his King.

CHAPTER 24

"Follow Me, Boys!"

Leading Dangerously

To visit Omaha Beach today is somewhat anticlimactic. The sloping cliffs that drift on to a serene seascape offer no hint as to the nightmare played out there on June 6, 1944, when thousands of men stormed out of the surf and into a hail of steel to find some tenuous refuge at the base of those bluffs.

Trapped in a pocket of relative safety, men quickly understood that their choices were limited to sure slaughter on the beach or probable slaughter on the cliffs. In time, here and there a gap was blown in the swirls of barbed wire opening the way through to a ravine or gully. It was here that real leadership was shown.

Someone, often a mere enlisted man would rise to his feet and shout "Follow me, boys!" and take off running through the breach toward danger and the unknown. Some of these leaders made it only a few steps. But enough of these incredible, mostly unknown men plowed through to make a difference and win the day.

In ages past, people were seemingly content to follow the command or directions of an appointed leader. Today, especially with the scent of skepticism many have about the genuineness of those who are connected to the church (including the leaders), the hallmark of authenticity is men and women who are able and willing to stand up and say, "Follow me."

Of course those two words typified many encounters with Jesus. So persuasive was His example and presence that He could simply say to a man, "Follow Me," and the guy would drop everything right in the middle of the workday and commit himself to a whole new lifestyle and Master.

Do what I do, model your life after mine, parrot my investments of time, energy, and money, put your heart where I put mine, handle issues the way I handle them, speak the way I speak, love the way I love. The apostle Paul said as much when he implored his readers to "Follow my example, as I follow the example of Christ" (1 Corinthians 11:1).

People need to catch their leaders leading the way toward an authentic Christian lifestyle. People need to follow them in humility by catching their leaders cleaning the toilets, washing the church van, or folding and labeling a newsletter. They need be able to follow them in loving, romantic marriages by catching the pastor holding hands with his spouse in public and snuggling with her in the booth at their favorite restaurant. They need to follow them as they live simply, generously, hospitably, and daringly. They need to follow them as they give away power, not hoard it.

As you probably know, the book *The Purpose-Driven Life* parked on the best-seller list for a long time. Millions of copies were sold, which, of course, translates into millions of dollars for the author, Pastor Rick Warren. And who are we to deny it to him? After all, he was sharp enough to create a book that moved and motivated people to such a degree that they snatched up extra copies to give to friends and spread, via word of mouth, the praises of this work. By the rules of hit-making in America, Rick is set for life, his kids can afford the best colleges money can buy, and his wife can buy an oceanfront home with all the servants to go with it.

After all, he earned it.

But earn it or not, what you probably don't know is that Rick won't be getting a penny from *The Purpose-Driven Life*. Rick has decided to give all the royalties to help fight AIDS in Africa.

Just because you can make millions doesn't mean you should spend it on your version of the American dream. Especially if you want to be able to say with authenticity, "Follow me, boys!" And if this is true of a pastor, it is just as true of anyone else in the fold.

Pastors and the churches that give them a paycheck often think they are paid to do things. They think they are paid to deliver sermons. They think they are paid to counsel people. They think they are paid to teach Bible studies or lead others to the Lord.

I think we would do better if we paid our leadership to empower other people to do things, especially if they are as capable or more capable to do the task than the pastor is.

Imagine if someone came into the church who was a wonderfully gifted speaker. Someone far more interesting and engaging than the pastor, someone who really connected and motivated people to follow Christ better. What chance do you think there would be of the pastor stepping aside and saying, "It is obvious that God has given you as a gift to our church. Please, the pulpit is yours as often as you would like it"?

Not much of a chance. Because the platform is power, and it takes an awful lot of security, faith, and trust to give up power. And besides, we are paying the pastor to speak and he should do so to prove he is worth his keep—even if he isn't that great at it.

I am a lousy counselor. Lousy—almost empty when it comes to empathy. Especially if someone comes to me with some massive bird's nest of a problem that is going to take months to work through. I figure that if you can't get it sorted out within the hour I'll give you a 39-cent bullet that can put you out of your misery.

Needless to say, the rest of the leadership team strongly suggests that I do very little counseling. And I am a happy guy because of this widely accepted personal limitation. Instead, we went out and found people in the church to whom God had given the gift of counseling, so we use them instead. (What a novel concept, using people's gifts for the best of the body.)

The same thing happens with me regarding control of money. All six of us church leaders took a poor man's personality test. I scored as an otter, monkey, chipmunk, or some other kind of playful animal. On the back of the test, under the animal that best described my personality type, it specifically warns, "This kind should not be allowed to handle money."

But we already knew that. ("If you have it, spend it!" that's my motto.)

Now, in a church, getting access to the money is another one of those power buttons. And we gave that power to a member of the team who would know when and where to push it. Once again, I am a happy guy because of it.

If we want our people for whom we have oversight—be they adults, teens, or kids—to live a life of challenge, adventure, and spiritual integrity, then there needs to be someone who will risk standing up and saying, "Follow me, boys!"

And even if we have not been designated with official leadership "rank," are we willing, when we spot a path through the maze and barbed wire of this life, to take the mantle of leadership afforded by the opportunity and rise to our feet to lead the way?

CHAPTER 25

Rites of Passage

Celebrating Milestones

The kids were pensive.

Outside, a cold drizzling rain was coating the pine trees with mist.

There were sixty of us, half men, half boys from ages twelve to fourteen, in the meeting hall of a camp at an altitude of 5,000 feet. The boys had come in response to a flyer advertising this weekend event with these simple words: *Leave a boy, return a man.* The men were there to help with that transformation.

The first evening meeting was drawing to a close. The men and their gear were warmly ensconced in a row of nearby cabins. The boys' gear sat in a pile under the eves of the meeting room.

Something was afoot. The boys could feel it. But it still came as a shock to them when I announced that the cabins were for *men* only and as they had not yet proven themselves to be worthy of the company of men, they would be given a few tarps, rope, and clothespins and could go off and try to get comfortable outside in the rain.

We locked the meeting room, our cars, and booted out every one of those shocked faces for a very uncomfortable night.

It was the opening round of a well-planned, but to the boys, secret ordeal, a church-sponsored rite of passage that would culminate in their becoming welcomed into manhood and the privileges and responsibilities that being a man of God entails.

Human beings seemed to be built to celebrate milestones. Ancient tribes created strange and bizarre rituals to mark the movement from one stage of human development to another.

The Lord gave the church the milestone of baptism to help connect the business of the heart with a tangible act, thus cementing the decision to be a disciple.

Over the years, the church enfolded other points of passage into her domain and created new ones. Marriage, death, birth: All are celebrated in some way or form by the community of faith.

I think this is a good thing, especially in a world that has drifted toward a weird form of homogenization that tries to pretend that cohabitation is the same as marriage, genders are neutral, and commitment to a standard is passé.

It is important and meaningful when the Christian community celebrates the significant crossings of life with each other. At our church we use the magic of the Internet to make everyone in the congregation aware of those little passages that are constantly taking place in the community of faith: birthdays, anniversaries, births. It's wonderful to hear people greet someone with "Happy Birthday!" because he was alerted to the occasion already via e-mail.

Perhaps it's time, as a Christian church family, to rethink our relationship to the milestones of life, to polish up or repair some that have been with us for a long time, and if possible, place a few more in the ground.

Maybe we should start with the covenant of marriage. While the whole idea of legal marriage is being assailed from all quarters and may end up being whatever two or more human beings want to define it to be, perhaps in the church we ought to be far more intentional and restrictive.

I agree with C. S. Lewis, who thought that there ought to be two different kinds of marriage. One was a "state" form of marriage, purely civil and run by whatever functionaries the state would appoint and liable to whatever rules the state imposes, and the other was "Christian" marriage, which comes with a whole vastly different set of values and expectations. As Lewis pointed out, the distinction should be quite clear.

Perhaps it would be good to up the ante for those desiring a Christian marriage. More premarriage counseling, tougher divorce requirements, and so on. Christians would be encouraged to celebrate a uniquely *Christian* marriage, and if they were wed in a civil ceremony, to redo their vows as Christians, with the support and guidance of a church congregation.

We could tinker with something as elementary as a Baby Dedication. This is typically something that the parents do to indicate that they are making a covenant with God to raise their offspring to serve and revere the Lord. But wouldn't it have more power if we could tweak the typical Baby Dedication into not only a covenant between parents and God but a covenant with the *church* to help the parents raise the child? Voluntary prayer warriors might come forward to follow this child into adulthood by bathing him with daily prayer. Real godparents might rise up to make sure that this child would be taught the gospel. Older couples might use the Baby Dedication as an opportunity to contact the parents and be part of their support team or their in-house grandparents.

But besides honoring those milestones we already have, perhaps we ought to actively consider encouraging our people to mark their passages with other kinds of ceremony.

One milestone might be some kind of "joining" to a community of faith. This could be the conscious choice going from being a watcher to a doer, an attendee to a participant, a taker to a giver. In some ways it could be like church membership . . . sorta.

Like many churches in the last decade or so, we have found a significant portion of our congregation extremely hesitant to formally commit to church membership. My parents and those of their generation were consummate joiners. Shriners, Boy Scouts, Bowling Club, church, you *joined up!* Their spawn have the opposite tendency. Attend, but be very cautious in commitment.

In most churches where voting is part of the process in getting things done and leaders are elected, one *must* be a member to vote. This usually entails some kind of membership class, avowing to the beliefs and standards of the particular church, and culminates in being presented to the congregation as a new member. But even these kinds of church governments are finding "joining" to be a hard sell to younger attendees.

One idea currently in our hatchery is something called *The*

Order of the Towel. An "order" would be like being in the Special Forces, or the Green Beret, of the church. It would be entirely voluntary but highly desirable—and challenging.

The Order of the Towel is based on the example of Jesus, who modeled servant leadership by washing the feet of the disciples: "So if I, the Master and Teacher, washed your feet, you must now wash each other's feet. I've laid down a pattern for you. What I've done, you do"(John 13:14-15, MSG). With this pattern, the new order sets the world on its head and holds that self-sacrifice and servanthood become the rhythm that one must willingly dance to if he or she is part of *The Order of the Towel.*

This milestone requires commitments mandated by Scripture, roles and responsibilities as a part of the local family of believers. It separates the halfhearted from the wholehearted. It doesn't have the feel or smell of typical church membership, and it would be celebrated as a passage.

But what if we got some real creative thinking going on the milestones of life and faith? What if we threw a party for folks when they first became grandparents or hit fifty? What if we set up a program with driving mentors to help kids learn to use a stick shift? (I don't know about you, but this was a scary milestone moment for me.)

With a little thought we can add layers of understanding and meaning to already established milestones. For example, our church has the world's largest baptismal font: the Pacific Ocean. We gather on a public beach wearing our swim trunks, and wade out into the surf with those who want to get baptized and give them the full treatment: salt water, waves, undertow, and sharks—and we haven't lost any yet. It's a pretty good milestone in and of itself.

Recently we added another layer to this spiritual rite of passage. Reading in some ancient church history that in some locales initiates were stripped almost naked to be baptized (kind of like those we baptize at the beach) and then given a new garment, representative of being "clothed in salvation" (see Isaiah 61:10) gave us a new idea. We had extra large purple (for royalty) beach towels created for each person to be baptized. On each towel is emblazoned *All things have been made new!—John 1:12*. The towel is held by a person in the local community of faith who has volunteered to be the guide, helper, teacher, and encourager of this new addition to the family. When the initiates stagger out of the water they are cloaked in the Royal Robes of God's family by the person who will be their accountability partner in the faith.

Locating and celebrating milestones not only reverberates with the human heart but it also involves the Christian community in those things that are the common experiences of the mortal world. Layer upon layer of meaning and teaching in a mix of old and new rituals. And besides all that, it gives the church another excuse to party!

CHAPTER 26

The Dreams of God

Celebrating Our Visionaries

Does God have dreams?

Around here we like to ask ourselves questions like that. Even if you can't come up with an answer it does get the imagination going. And it leads to other musings. Such as: Does God *give* dreams to mere mortals like us? Dreams that may seem small on the surface but go miles deep. Dreams that are in full color, dreams that leave you wondering if it is still sleep or if it is the real thing, dreams that are like God: wild, creative, imaginative, original, complex, and wonderful.

And if God does give His people dreams, where are our dreamers? Why are there so few of them? And why does it seem that much of what passes for creativity is really just a spiritually souped-up clone of something secular culture is offering up?

I have a guess as to what happened to the dreamers.

We crushed them. We strangled their dreams with rolls and

rolls of red tape or suffocated them in the grip of unimaginative committees.

We stopped our ears to their dreams and told them they were unrealistic.

We adopted the role of Joseph's brothers and sneered sarcastically, "Here comes the dreamer!"

It is a terrible thing to crush a dream. It not only knocks the breath from dreamers, it sucks out their soul.

My stepfather, Paul Launer, was a baseball fanatic. He ate, drank, and breathed the game. His free time was spent on the sandlot, the Little League field, in the batting cage, and pitching balls in the middle of the street.

By his teen years he was a talent to behold. His fireball pitching got faster and faster and his accuracy continued to improve.

It was his seventeenth year; Paul played ball in the upper division of Little League. During one pivotal game, he was knocking out his opponents 1-2-3, inning after inning.

Unknown to him, sitting in the bleachers that afternoon was a scout from the Boston Red Sox.

Even though the rest of Paul's team was somewhat lackluster, the scout knew raw talent when he saw it—and he saw it in the arm of that young pitcher. While the game was still in progress, and without introducing himself, he asked the coach about the boy on the mound.

"What's that kid's name?" asked the scout.

"He's Paul Launer," rolled back the coach.

"How old is the boy?" responded the scout.

"Seventeen," said the coach.

The scout paused for a moment and then pulled out a small pad and pencil and asked, "Do ya know how I can contact his Pop?"

"Sure," replied the coach and with a few numbers given, the scout quietly returned to the bleachers.

A few days later, while Paul's father was shooting the breeze with some friends at his workplace, he got a surprise visitor.

It was the Boston Red Sox scout.

The scout shook the hand of the elder Launer and quickly tendered a card showing his credentials. "I've seen your boy in action," the scout said with a bright smile, "and I do believe he may have a future in the game of baseball."

Mr. Launer was taken aback for a moment by the shocking revelation of this unexpected visitor. He studied the card and glanced up at the scout. Then his face soured. "Naaaw!" the man slowly drawled. "He'd never make the grade."

"Well, sir, we would like a chance to find out," gently tossed back the Red Sox scout. "But since he is only seventeen, we will need you to sign for him."

Mr. Launer was silent for a moment, and then, leaning both hands on the shop counter, and with pursed lips and a lowered, shaking head, he replied slowly, "No, I don't think so. I appreciate the interest and all, but I just don't think the boy has what it takes."

The scout, puzzled that any all-American father would pass on having his boy play professional baseball, thanked the elder Launer for his time and left the shop.

Paul's father briefly discussed his reasoning to the stunned friends who had overheard the whole exchange and then went home that night and never spoke to Paul of the visitor he had talked to that day.

Several months later, one of Paul's father's friends accidentally let the cat out of the bag.

"What? What was that? Dad, a scout came to see you?" Paul asked in bewilderment.

"Yeah," his father replied without offering any more explanation.

"Is it . . . is it true you wouldn't sign for me?" asked the now obviously agitated boy.

"Look, Son, I didn't want to see you get disappointed when you didn't make it," said his dad defensively.

Paul's voice rose almost hysterically. "Disappointed? This was my chance, Dad! This was my dream, and you didn't think I was good enough to at least try for it?!"

Paul's heart was completely crushed, the flame in his young spirit extinguished by his own father.

Paul became a self-fulfilling prophecy of his father's opinion of him and worked most of his life in a hum-drum, unchallenging job. But the wound his father had inflicted turned poisonous, and in his own words Paul said, "From that day on I hated my father with all my heart. It was only finding Christ twenty years later that made it possible for me to forgive him."

Over the years the Christian church hasn't done much better with our dreamers.

We have scoffed at their ridiculous ideas.

We have implied they may be spiritually contaminated, theologically compromised, or heretically inclined.

We have sent them through a labyrinth of committees only to table their ideas to another time.

We have even assigned them to the dustbin of utopian loonies.

But every once in a while one escapes and becomes a St. Francis of Assisi, a Bunyan, a Wycliffe, or a Mother Teresa. Every once in a while one of them actually refuses to let their God-instilled dreams be crushed and creates a wondrous song, magnificent art, a liberating and attractive community of faith. Once someone actually achieves his or her dream it gives permission, even expectation, to others that their dreams have a shot at becoming reality.

A few years ago some of the high school kids decided to form a band in order to play for the local school talent contest. The problem was that they had no place to practice. Because they all went to our church they asked if they could hold band practice at our site.

"Sure," we said, and thought no more about it until one of the leadership team happened to be doing some work on campus during their practice session.

"Have you heard those kids?" he asked us. "They sound terrific!"

A few of us managed to stumble in on them practicing and we all agreed; these kids were great!

Someone offered to record a couple of their original songs using the church gear. Someone else, who had a couple of connections in the Christian music world, offered to send a copy to a label. Before the band could blink they were asked to sign a contract and go to California for a recording session. The kids asked if they could wait until summer break so they didn't have to miss school.

In the end, the band made four albums, toured every state in the Union at least twice, brought to the label another band from the church, and made every group of young musicians think that the course set by their predecessors is the natural order of things.

Dreaming big seems easy when you see sweet results for other dreamers.

Perhaps if we, as a church, spent a bit more time listening to our dreamers and helping them to decide if their dreams are God-breathed ideas or wishful thinking it would have big payoffs.

Perhaps if the church were to recast itself into a place of possibilities for dreamers we would attract and discover more of them. Wouldn't it be great if part of the signage of churches everywhere was "Dreamers Welcome Here"?

Perhaps if we welcomed and even celebrated true visionaries and banished from our church vocabulary the phrase "we never did it that way before," we might wake up one day to find that by dreaming the dreams of God we had started fulfilling the dreams of God.

CHAPTER 27

The Gum of God

A Legacy That Sticks

I have never been able to figure out how gum ends up on a hot asphalt parking lot. Does the gum suddenly leap from open mouths? Do people spit it out the window as some kind of insult to the establishment they have just visited prior to driving away? Are we talking about a race of slobs who can't chew the stuff long enough to reach a trash can? Is it merely the result of children who can't jabber and chew gum at the same time, or is the problem from beings more intentional and dark-hearted who know they are laying clingy traps for some unsuspecting traveler?

It remains a deep mystery to me. But the end result of a gob of gum roasting away on warm asphalt is not a mystery to any of us.

There I am minding my own business, reviewing the "Honey Do" list I have been given as I head from the parking lot into the store and wham! My determined tread is interrupted by the pull of something rooted in the ground. If I am wearing the typical

Hawaiian footwear, rubber slippers, I may end up suddenly shoe-less. And let's not even mention the disgusting circumstances if I hit that booby trap in bare feet.

A wad of gum has got me.

I lift my shoe to find a sticky lump attached to the sole of my shoe and another fragment clinging to the ground with a spiderweb of extra sticky stuff in between, all of which has been spending intimate time in some stranger's mouth.

Hostile words spring from my lips! I have been ambushed by an obnoxious roadside bomb that has been simmering in the hot sun for who knows how long waiting just for me!

The "Honey Do" list is forgotten! I dance on one foot and try to find something to scrape away the offending mass.

But you can never seem to get it all and I walk into the store awkwardly feeling the remains of a lump of goo that once enter-tained someone else trying to make itself a permanent part of my shoe.

I was thinking the other day, what if money were sticky? What if instead of stumbling into someone's sticky gum, I stumbled onto someone's lost money? Would it bug me to feel a wadded up twenty-dollar bill under my foot? Would I be annoyed at hav-ing to stop and peel ten spots off the sole of my shoe? Heck no! Going over the hot asphalt would be a treasure hunt instead of a minefield. Would I be cursing the cretin who discarded his cash? No way! Bring on the cretins! (You see how my mind works; these things just show up in the brain cavity, it's not as if I don't have anything better to think about.)

It also gave me a fitting (although slightly weird) analogy of the work that a church is to do in a community.

You see, we don't always know the results of our labor, actions, or investment. God deals in vast quantities of time but we like to see our spiritual deals culminated in a moment—or at least by the end of the retreat. And God is not in a rush to do His business in the hearts of people. He takes His time even with the runaways and those we figure are a lost cause.

I have on my desk a letter from a man who, for a brief moment of time two decades ago, was part of a youth group I led. The letter writer describes how, as a young teen from a secular home, he had stumbled into some nutty activity put on by the youth department and ended up giving his life to Christ. As he tells it, his later teen years were filled with bad choices he *knew* were bad choices because of his early experience with the Lord. Yet he drifted away and ultimately got sucked into the party scene until the party moved on without him and he was left paying a lifetime bill.

But underneath it all, there was something stuck to his soul.

After a number of years in the wilderness, with his relationships stretched taut and his ability to reign in his urges in tatters, the ember of a faith long ago abandoned became the only source of genuine warmth left in his life. He began the long, difficult but healing journey back to the faith he had started as a young teen. In time, he was able to beat his demons, restore his family, and become an active leader in his local church. He tracked me down to tell me his story and say thank you. It was a wonderful gift.

But his story had little to do with me. It was the glorious gum of God. Something good that stuck to the boy and tracked with him through years of misery into revitalized adulthood.

It gives me great joy to know that something God does through us in a moment of time often has an echo that reaches to eternity. And it is wonderful to be part of something that really and truly makes a difference in the life and destiny of another human being.

This is the wonderful legacy of a community of faith. Our leaders may disappear; our messages, even the good ones with lots of cool object lessons, visuals, and stories will dissolve; our events, worship services, and mission activities will be forgotten. Our churches may even close. But the globs of genuine love, the gum of God's truth, mercy, forgiveness, and sacrifice for mankind remain and are next to impossible to scrape off a soul.

It is the best we can hope for: that our churches, our family, and our own actions will litter the terrain we tramp upon with small bits of benevolence and eternal hope. That those who have contact with our people, with our leadership, with our endeavors will tread upon something that will be hard to shake, noticeable in their souls, and so annoying, in a wonderful way, that they will one day have to stop and deal with it.

And that, in the end, is what I hope for in this book. That something divine might have plopped out in the pages. My hope is that a little sticky astonishing something, direct from the Father of Lights, would have squeezed past all the human elements, earthbound foolishness, and moral frailties and made its way underfoot.

I truly hope that you have stepped in the gum of God.

ENDNOTE

1. Samuel Hopkins, *The Life and Character of Jonathan Edwards*, published in 1765.

ABOUT THE AUTHOR

Rick Bundschuh is a pastor, veteran youth worker, writer, speaker, and cartoonist based in Kauai, Hawaii.

Born and raised in a fifties-era stucco house near the ocean in San Diego, California, Rick came of age in the surfer/hippie culture of the sixties.

Fortunate enough to connect with an aggressive and imaginative youth pastor during his early teen years, Rick converted to Christianity (from raw hedonism) and began the spiritual journey that, along the way, led him into the ministry.

After attending Capernwray Bible School in the United Kingdom, Rick became a youth pastor himself, continuing in that calling for the next twenty-eight years, with the exception of a six-year stint as the Creative Director for Youth Resources at Gospel Light Publications. Known for his creativity, "over the top" imagination, and successful efforts in reaching unchurched teens, Rick has been instrumental in flooding the churches he's worked in with pagans, trolls, and other wild converts (a talent not appreciated in all circles).

Along the way he managed to squeeze out a regular two-page cartoon feature in *Surfer Magazine* (running 1980–1986) and authored dozens of books. He continues to write and illustrate material for various publishers.

Migrating to Kauai in 1986 (rumors he was chased out of California are unfounded) Rick soon found himself back in youth ministry. Currently Rick serves as a teaching pastor at Kauai Christian Fellowship, which was founded by Rick and a few other "mad hatters" in 1991. KCF is a nondenominational church with a reputation for being high energy, amplified, and postmodern oriented.

Rick lives with his beautiful wife, Lauren, their kids, Mason, Justin, Allegra, and Hudson, a wienie dog named Rachel, and a quiver of surfboards in Kalaheo, Hawaii.

MORE RESOURCES TO CHALLENGE THE CHURCH

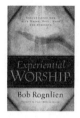

Experiential Worship

Bob Rognlien   1-57683-663-0

Provocative and practical, this book centers worship on Jesus' Great Commandment: to love God with everything you are. Build a more effective and heartfelt worship service that churches of all sizes will be able to implement for years to come.

Reclaiming God's Original Intent for the Church

Wes Roberts and Glenn Marshall   1-57683-407-7

By getting back to core values and away from energy-sapping obsessions, pastors learn how the focused, agile small church is the past—and the future—of the church.

Dangerous Wonder

Mike Yaconelli   1-57683-128-0

If you're looking for the joy and freedom of faith, this book will open your eyes and your life to the exciting adventure of a relationship with God.

To order copies, visit your local Christian bookstore,
call NavPress at 1-800-366-7788, or log on to www.navpress.com.
To locate a Christian bookstore near you,
call 1-800-991-7747.

BRINGING TRUTH TO LIFE
www.navpress.com